# Teaching Behavioral Self-Control
# to Students

# Teaching Behavioral Self-Control to Students

Edward A. Workman

*University of Tennessee at Chattanooga*

PRO-ED
"Services for Professional Educators"
5341 Industrial Oaks Blvd.
Austin, Texas 78735

PRO-ED
5341 Industrial Oaks Blvd.
Austin, Texas 78735

**Library of Congress Cataloging in Publication Data**

Workman, Edward, 1952–
    Teaching behavioral self-control to students.

    Includes bibiographical references and indexes.
    1. Learning disabilities.  2. Self-control—Study
and teaching.  3. Behavior modification.  I. Title.
LC4704.W68          371.9′043                    82-435
ISBN 0–936104–23–6            AACR2

10  9  8  7  6  5  4  3  2      86  85  84  83

# Table of Contents

# Figures

# Preface

The public education system in the United States is currently being forced to cope with a number of powerful external pressures. Two in particular seem to place severe stress on those concerned with the quality of education. Dwindling state and federal revenues are forcing schools to reduce, and in some cases terminate, many crucial support services. At the same time, public demand is increasing for schools to socialize children more effectively, as well as educate them. In order to adapt to such pressures, schools must use methods which foster the socialization of children in a cost-effective manner. That is, schools must use methods which are consistently effective, but do not rely excessively on complex programs requiring highly sophisticated and costly personnel.

The field of applied behavior analysis, or **behavior modification,** has generated a number of socialization and education technologies which are highly cost effective. These technologies fall under the rubric of behavioral self-control. They are cost-effective because their implementation and operation relies upon the resources of sudents rather than adults, and because they provide teachers with efficient and streamlined methods for improving the social and academic behaviors of students.

In addition to being cost-effective, behavioral self-control technologies provide students with skills which will be useful throughout their lives. These skills will enable students to function as independent, self-managed adults, who can use their own resources to cope with life's demands. After all, it would seem that the ultimate goal of all education efforts is to enable students to become independent and self-managed citizens.

This book was written to provide teachers with the skills for teaching behavioral self-control to their students. Those who read and use the book will find behavioral self-control to be a refreshing, effective, and positive technology for transforming students into more fully-functioning and responsible adults.

# Acknowledgments

I would like to acknowledge the contributions of the following persons: my wife, Brooks, for her extreme patience, encouragement, and understanding during the production of this book; Debbie Edgemon, for secretarial and editorial assistance far above the call of duty; my mentors, Donald Dickinson and Robert L. Williams at the University of Tennessee–Knoxville; and my colleagues at the University of Tennessee–Chattanooga, for their reinforcement, punishment, prompting, modeling, and overall stimulation—Ralph Hood, Paul Watson, Edward Green, George Helton, and Ron Morris.

# Introduction

This book is about Behavioral Self Control (BSC). Specifically, it's about how students can learn to use BSC in order to improve their performance in the classroom.

As you will see more clearly in subsequent chapters of this book, there are three main types of BSC which students can use to modify their own behavior. You are probably quite familiar with behavior modification procedures where the teacher, or some other adult, modifies a student's behavior through techniques like prompting, fading, modeling, and positive reinforcement. BSC represents an extension of these techniques. However, with BSC, it is the student, rather than an adult, who *eventually* carries out the techniques to modify his or her own behavior.

The purpose of the book is to show adults how they can teach BSC to students. You will learn how to implement a wide array of BSC programs with students in classroom settings, and more importantly, you will learn to teach the students to implement and use these programs to improve their own classroom behavior.

There is often some confusion regarding what the term classroom behavior actually means. For purposes of this book, it refers to any *significant action* in which a student might engage in the classroom. This includes positive behaviors we would like to encourage, such as paying attention, working appropriately in one's seat, participating in class discussions, reading assignments, working on math problems, taking quizzes, and turning in homework. It also includes negative behaviors we would like to observe less often, such as leaving one's seat without permission, talking without permission, disruptively jumping from one activity to another, making many errors on assignments or not turning in assignments at all, or acting aggressively toward others.

In this book, you will learn to teach students BSC procedures for increasing positive behaviors and decreasing negative behaviors. You will learn to teach students procedures they can use to improve their behavior in the classroom. You will also learn to show students how to improve their ability to function effectively as mature human beings, capable of managing their own behavior and their own lives!

The primary audience for this book is the classroom teacher in either regular or special education/resource settings. As a person on the "front lines" of education, who has daily contact with students, a teacher has the best opportunity for teaching BSC skills.

The material in this book will allow the teacher to teach BSC skills to students in every grade level, from kindergarten to grade 12. The material is also applicable with students at every developmental level, from the developmentally delayed to the extremely bright. The ability to manage one's own behavior is both desirable and possible for essentially every student. And, for that reason, this book will have maximum benefit if it is used by classroom teachers. After all, they represent that group in direct contact with the most students.

This book will also be useful to those who work with classroom teachers. Many who provide support services to the classroom will find material they can use in a consultative capacity. Such persons include school psychologists, consulting teachers, school counselors, educational diagnosticians, behavior specialists, and school principals.

This book is organized around the following three basic components of BSC: SA, SM, and SR.

Chapter I, The Rationale for Teaching BSC, provides a general theoretical overview of the use of BSC in classroom settings. First it attempts to clarify how BSC is related to those procedures traditionally referred to as behavior modification. It then presents the reasons why educators should want students to learn BSC skills. The chapter concludes with a relatively detailed discussion of the specific types of student behaviors that can be improved via BSC.

Chapter I, Principles and Techniques of BSC, provides a detailed presentation of the three basic components and the specific techniques which comprise each component. Each technique is discussed, along with the research demonstrating its usefulness in classroom settings. No attempt is made to provide an exhaustive research review. Instead, representative studies on each technique are presented. An attempt is made to show the reader that BSC is effective with students in a wide range of age and ability levels. The chapter concludes with an expanded glossary of all BSC techniques to be used in this book.

Each of the book's three final chapters is devoted to one of these components. The chapters begin with a step-by-step guide to implementation, and then present case studies from actual classrooms, demonstrating the use and potential of techniques derived from the BSC component. It should be noted that the case studies represent BSC programs as conducted in actual classrooms. They in no way attempt to attain a high level of experimental control or rigor. Most of the data on which the case studies are based were obtained from observations by the author's student assistants, and some are based on the observations of teachers or aides.

Chapter II, Self-Assessment, describes a number of techniques wherein students learn to effectively evaluate and guide their own behavior. Three **Self-Assessment** techniques provide the focus of the chapter: **Self-Ratings, Self-Instruction Training**, and Verbal Mediation Training. Each technique is presented in terms of step-by-step methods for implementation. Actual case studies exemplifying each technique are also presented.

In Chapter IV, Self-Monitoring, techniques are presented in which students monitor and record their own behavior, and then chart (on graphs) their performance. These techniques result in improvements in student behavior by enhancing students' awareness of their behavior and providing them with clear feedback on improvements. Two **Self-Monitoring** techniques are presented in detail: **Frequency Self-Monitoring** and **Interval Self-Monitoring**. Specific, step-by-step instructions and classroom case studies are provided for each.

Chapter V, Self-Reinforcement, focuses on techniques in which students positively reinforce themselves for engaging in appropriate behaviors, or for not engaging in appropriate behaviors. Different types of self-reinforcers (e.g., points, tokens, positive fantasies) are discussed in some detail, as are methods for determining "back-up" reinforcers for use in Self-Reinforcement program.s As in previous chapters, step-by-step instructions and case study materials are presented.

# Teaching Behavioral Self-Control to Students

# I
# The Rationale for Teaching Behavioral Self-Control (BSC)

## BEHAVIOR MODIFICATION: THE FULL STORY

Most readers are familiar with the set of principles and techniques called **behavior modification** (Kazdin, 1980; Clarizio, 1980). To most, it refers to the use of external methods of influencing student behavior. Some of these methods are now "household words" among those working in educational settings. They include, but are not limited to, the following:

**Positive Reinforcement.** Providing students with desirable events, like praise or free time, contingent upon appropriate behavior.

**Time Out.** Removing a student from a reinforcing environment contingent upon inappropriate behavior, such as removing a student from recess for 10 minutes following fighting behavior.

**Response Cost.** Removing rewards from a student contingent upon inappropriate behavior, such as removing 10 minutes of free time due to talking out inappropriately.

**Prompting.** Setting up a situation so that appropriate behavior is likely to occur, for example, by giving clear instructions.

**Fading.** Slowly removing prompts or contingencies after a student's behavior has improved to the extent desired, for example, using a free time reward system less and less often after behavior has improved.

**Modeling.** Focusing a student's attention on examples of appropriate behavior, like pointing out how certain peers are behaving appropriately.

Over a decade of applied research has shown that these and other behavior modification methods are highly effective in improving students' social and academic behavior (Kazdin, 1980; Williams & Anandam, 1973; Clarizio, 1980).

As previously suggested, most people view behavior modification as a set of external methods, methods that the teacher (an agent external to the student) uses to improve student behavior. This notion has been supported by the fact that early classroom behavior modification efforts focused almost entirely on the use of external control techniques (Williams & Anandam, 1973). More recently, however, behavior modification research has expanded the field to include methods whereby students can control their own behavior (Clarizio, 1980).

In a recent description of the behavior modification process, Walker (1979) noted three distinct phases, which clearly demonstrate the broad nature of contemporary behavior modification.

During **Phase I**, the classroom teacher implements positive reinforcement procedures to improve student behavior. For example, students might receive points and praise for being "on-task" during classroom assignments, or for completing a given number of assignment items correctly. The earned points might be exchanged for free time at the end of the class period, or for some other reinforcing agents.

In addition to positive reinforcement, the teacher may use additional procedures such as **response cost**, for example, loss of points for out-of-seat or other inappropriate behavior; **prompting**, for example, writing clear instructions and rules on the board and periodically reminding students to stay on-task; and **modeling**, for example, pointing out those students who are on-task most of the time.

Once desired student behavior changes are attained, **Phase II** is implemented. This entails transferring control of Phase I procedures to the students themselves. In other words, students are taught to monitor their own behavior and reinforce themselves for appropriate behaviors, like being "on-task." These procedures fall into the domain of **Behavioral Self Control**. During Phase II, the same procedures as found in Phase I are used, but it is the students, not the teacher, who actually implement and administer the procedures.

As the final step in the behavior change process, **Phase III** involves the "fading out" of all systematic behavior control techniques. The procedures wherein students reinforce themselves for appropriate behavior are slowly removed, and control is shifted to reinforcers that occur naturally in the students' environment, like social status, grades, and achievement feedback. The three phases of this overall behavior change process are shown in Figure 1.

**Figure 1**
**The Behavior Change Process**

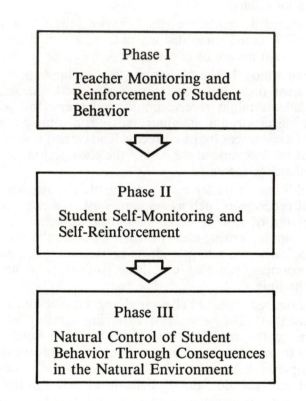

Phase I

Teacher Monitoring and
Reinforcement of Student
Behavior

Phase II

Student Self-Monitoring and
Self-Reinforcement

Phase III

Natural Control of Student
Behavior Through Consequences
in the Natural Environment

Walker's (1979) three-phase model tells the full story of behavior modification. It points out that student self-control is just as important, and as much a part of behavior modification, as the teacher's control of student behavior. Throughout the rest of this chapter, and, for that matter, the remainder of the book, we'll explore the use of Behavioral Self-Control with students. As indicated in the introduction, this book assumes that the reader is familiar with traditional external behavior modification procedures. The reader who wants a refresher in this area could start with the excellent texts by Kazdin (1980), Clarizio (1980), or Long and Frye (1977), all of which provide a detailed discussion of the elementary principles of behavior modification.

## WHY TEACH BSC

The following sections explore the rationale behind the use of Behavioral Self-Control (BSC) during **Phase II** of the behavior modification process. We'll take a look at the various reasons educators should concern themselves with teaching self-control to students.

Although the benefits of BSC are numerous, we'll focus on the three most important to educators: (1) the fact that teachers will not always be around to guide students by providing consistent feedback about their behavior; (2) the need for students to learn to take responsibility for their own behavior; and (3) the need to insure that the effects of traditional external behavior modification programs (Phase I) not only have positive effects in many settings, but also last for prolonged periods.

### The Teacher Won't Always Be Around

Effective traditional behavior modification programs are characterized by **consistent behavior contingencies** (Clarizio, 1980; Williams & Anandam, 1973). In other words, there exists a clear relation between (1) appropriate student behavior and reinforcing consequences and (2) inappropriate behavior and negative consequences (punishment). When students are behaving appropriately, the teacher administers **immediate** praise and/or tangible rewards, like points or tokens which can be exchanged for rewards. When students are behaving inappropriately, the teacher administers immediate negative consequences, like time out or response cost. A classroom environment characterized by such immediate consequences, consistently applied, results in high rates of appropriate social and academic behavior. In other words, under such conditions, students learn rapidly!

The world outside the classroom is also characterized by behavioral contingencies. It is true that certain behaviors are rewarded, while others are punished. However, a major difference between the outside world and the classroom which uses behavior modification is that the former does not always provide consistent and immediate consequences. For example, the rewards we receive are, hopefully, consistent, but certainly not immediate. Most people work for two to four weeks before being reinforced with a paycheck. Also, the social praise we receive for doing a really good job is neither immediate nor consistent. Most people are not rewarded by praise and social status each time they do something outstanding. Furthermore, outstanding performances are often not followed by immediate rewards.

This lack of consistent and immediate environmental feedback on our performance makes it necessary for us to provide ourselves with our own feedback. When our teachers are no longer with us, are no longer available to guide our behavior via reinforcement, we must be able to reinforce ourselves. You might say that the process of growing up requires that we become less and less dependent upon the feedback of others and more dependent on the feedback we give ourselves.

Behavioral Self-Control (BSC) provides the feedback not always provided by our environment (Workman & Hector, 1978). BSC can "make up" for otherwise inconsistent and delayed reinforcers from our environment. We all regularly take advantage of this principle when we praise ourselves for some excellent performance. Our praise mitigates the delay between our performance and eventual reinforcement. That is, our self-praise makes the inevitable delays in our reinforcers a little more tolerable. It also keeps us from simply "giving up" in the face of sparse reinforcement.

By teaching self-control skills to students, we provide them with the ability to give themselves feedback on their own behavior. We teach them to monitor and evaluate their own actions and to systematically reinforce themselves for productive and effective actions. We teach them to function productively when the teacher is no longer around! This process is shown graphically in Figure 2.

**Figure 2**
**The Effect of BSC on Students' Productive**
**and Independent Behavior**

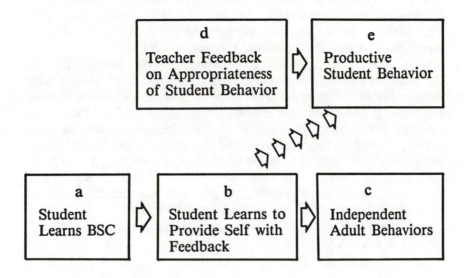

Robert Gagne (1965), the eminent educational psychologist, once said that the ultimate goal of all education is to wean students progressively from dependence upon teachers and teach them to do what is necessary to guide their own behavior, to teach themselves in other words. Perhaps BSC provides educators with the best available method to accomplish this noble goal.

## Learning to Take Responsibility

Perhaps one of the most ubiquitous goals in education is to teach children to take responsibility for their own actions. One reason for this is that the society in which we live expects schools to teach children to take responsibility (and be responsible citizens), as well as to read, write and compute solutions to math problems.

Taking responsibility is related to a concept called **locus of control**. Locus of control refers to an individual's perceptions of what causes his or her behavior (Williams & Long, 1979). An individual is said to have an **external locus of control** if he or she perceives actions (and fate) to be the result of external forces. These external forces might include other people in authority or random events. Individuals who feel this way believe they have very little to do about what happens to them. They literally see themselves as pawns of external circumstances!

A person is said to have an **internal locus of control** if actions are perceived to be the result of forces within. Such people view themselves as the ultimate cause of what happens to them. Instead of viewing themselves as pawns of external events, they view external events as being under their own control, at least to some extent. Whether their actions lead to rewards or punishments, people with an internal locus of control view their own behavior as the ultimate source, the ultimate cause, of these rewards and punishments. In other words, people with an internal locus of control take responsibility for their own behavior!

The relation between internal and external locus of control is shown in Figure 3.

**Figure 3**
**The Effect of Locus of Control on Motivation**

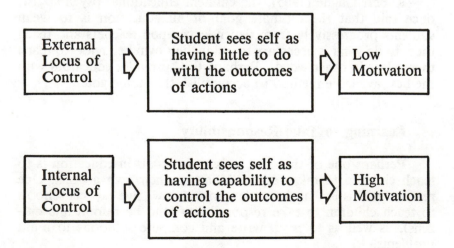

Students who have an internal locus of control are going to be substantially more motivated than are those with an external locus of control. Why? Think about it! If you believe you have the capability for accomplishing something, you're going to be more motivated to accomplish it than if you see yourself as having little, if any, chance of accomplishment. Students with an internal locus of control believe in themselves and their ability to make things happen! More specifically, they believe that it is their own actions which make things happen, not random events or powerful authority figures. Therefore, they are more motivated to take positive actions toward accomplishing their goals.

There is evidence that BSC moves students in the direction of an internal locus of control. In a study conducted by Pawlicki (1976), students learned techniques of BSC and completed projects where they actually modified their own behavior. Over a relatively short period of time, these students became more internal in their locus of control.

In a study reported by Bradley and Gaa (1977), students (1) received feedback regarding their academic performance, (2) set clear goals for the coming week, and (3) discussed ways of attaining their goals. As a result the students began to see themselves as being more in control of their academic achievement. They internalized their locus of control and began to take responsibility for their own actions!

## Maintenance and Generalization of Behavior Changes

As you remember, Phase I of the behavior change process involves the use of **external contingencies** to improve students' behavior. Students are reinforced by the teacher for appropriate behavior or approximations of appropriate behavior. Quite clearly, such external procedures can result in dramatic improvements in student behavior (Kazdin, 1980). However, Phase I procedures alone are frequently characterized by a lack of maintenance and generalization.

**Maintenance** refers to the extent to which changes in a student's behavior maintain over time, or how long the changes last. As a number of studies have shown (Marholin & Steinman, 1977; O'Leary, Becker, Evans, & Saudargas, 1969), a student's behavior may initially improve with the use of Phase I procedures, but then may revert to initial "pre-intervention" levels after the procedures are terminated. In other words, the behavior changes do not maintain or last over time.

As Kazdin (1980) has pointed out, BSC represents one of several effective methods for dealing with this problem. As an example, take the study by Wood and Flynn (1978). It involved a token reinforcement program wherein six disruptive male adolescents were reinforced for various appropriate social and academic behavior. Following appropriate behavior, these students received tokens which they could exchange for various privileges. After the program was instituted, there was a dramatic improvement in the students' behavior. However, when the tokens were no longer administered, the improvements were partially lost. The students' behavior reverted to levels similar to that found prior to the program. Following this reversal effect, Wood and Flynn (1978) implemented a BSC program. Not only did BSC result in improvements equal to those obtained with token reinforcement, but the effects were maintained after the BSC program was terminated.

It seems likely that the maintenance enhancement effect of BSC stems from students internalizing the BSC techniques. When students are being reinforced by their teacher, they are well aware that the reinforcement is coming from outside themselves. However, when students use BSC, they are reinforcing themselves. Not only does this help them learn appropriate behaviors (i.e., those being reinforced), but it allows them to learn the actual reinforcement operations. This gives them the opportunity to internalize the process of reinforcement of appropriate behavior. This process may, therefore, become a normal part of each student's "personality."

Once the student has acquired the habit of **self-reinforcement of appropriate behavior,** the termination of external teacher reinforcement is no longer crucial. Under such circumstances, students provide their own reinforcements.

**Generalization** refers to the extent to which student behavior changes transfer from one setting or situation to another. As Walker and Buckley (1972) have noted, Phase I behavior change procedures sometimes fail to produce this effect. For example, following **external** reinforcement for appropriate reading behaviors, a student might improve her "studying" behavior in reading class, but her "studying" behavior might remain unchanged during history class.

The very nature of BSC suggests that it can be useful in solving the generalization problems of Phase I procedures. With

BSC, students are controlling their own behavior. As a result, they are less dependent upon external support, that is, the teacher's reinforcement. If teacher reinforcement is available in one setting but not another, but it may make little difference, since it is **self-reinforcement** that affects the students' behavior.

An example of how BSC can be used to obtain behavior change generalization is found in a study conducted by Bornstein and Quevillon (1976). These researchers trained three pre-schoolers to use a BSC technique to increase their on-task behavior, in this case, paying attention. BSC training took place in a room outside the classroom, where the teacher was not present. When students returned to the classroom their on-task behavior improved dramatically, even though no systematic behavior change procedures were in effect. BSC produced behavior changes which automatically generalized or transferred from the training room to the regular classroom.

It seems clear that BSC represents an effective means of enhancing the maintenance and generalization of improvements in students' behavior. By teaching students to control their own behavior, the teacher provides them with a mechanism for behaving appropriately and productively in situations where teacher reinforcement support is minimal or absent. In other words, BSC provides students with a means of functioning at their best in the "real" world.

## CLASSROOM PROBLEMS BSC CAN ADDRESS

As Workman and Hector (1978) have pointed out, BSC procedures can be used to improve three types of student behaviors of concern to educators. These include on-task behavior, disruptive behavior, and academic product behaviors.

### On-task behavior

On-task behavior refers to a class of student behaviors which are extremely important for adaptation in the classroom. Generally, it involves behaviors which are considered to be pre-requisites for academic learning. These behaviors must occur if a student is to benefit from classroom experiences.

Most definitions of on-task behaviors include the following:

1. The student is looking at the teacher while the teacher is demonstrating a task, showing pictures, or working problems on the board.

2. The student is looking at and listening to the teacher while instructions are given.

3. The student is working on an assignment as directed by the teacher.

4. The student complies with specific instructions given by the teacher.

5. The student is looking at materials toward which the teacher directs his or her attention.

BSC has been shown to be useful in increasing the occurrence of on-task behaviors such as these (Workman & Hector, 1978). And, as a student's on-task behaviors increase, it stands to reason the student will perform more successfully on academic tasks.

### Disruptive behaviors

Disruptive behaviors are those which disrupt the on-going, appropriate performance of other students or that of the student who is behaving disruptively. These behaviors are incompatible with proper learning conditions.

Most definitions of disruptive behaviors include the following student actions:

1. The student repetitively makes noises which can be heard by other students.

2. The student leaves his or her seat or assigned area without permission.

3. The student talks out without permission.

4. The student threatens others verbally.

5. The student physically attacks others.

Research has shown that BSC techniques can be used to decrease the occurrence of disruptive behaviors, thereby improving students' school performance (Workman & Hector, 1978).

In most cases, BSC is used to increase behaviors which are incompatible with disruptive behavior, thus indirectly reducing disruption. For example, a student might learn to use BSC to stay in her seat and raise her hand for permission to talk. As BSC increases this student's in-seat and hand-raising behaviors, out-of-seat and talking-out behaviors will automatically decrease, since the two sets of behavior are incompatible with each other. They all simply cannot occur at the same time!

### Academic product behaviors

These refer to completed products which represent the end result of a student's on-task behavior. These behaviors are most highly valued by the educational community because they represent evidence that the student has learned something.

Common examples of academic product behaviors include the following:

1. The number of math homework problems solved correctly.

2. The number of correct items on a math test.

3. The number of correct sentences a student has written in a story.

4. The number of correctly spelled words on a list written by the student.

5. The number of questions a student can answer correctly after reading a passage from a story.

Both Workman and Hector (1978) and Peirsel and Kratochwill (1979) have presented convincing evidence that BSC is highly effective in increasing students' academic product behaviors. In other words, BSC has been shown to be effective in enhancing student achievement.

## THE COMPONENTS OF BSC

So far we've discussed BSC procedures in general terms. In this section, we'll take a closer look at what BSC is all about, examining those components which can be trained. We will explore the BSC skills which you can teach your students. The purpose of this exploration is to familiarize you with BSC techniques. A more detailed analysis will be provided in the next and subsequent chapters.

Glynn, Thomas, and Shee (1973) identified three basic components of BSC. These components include the following:

1. Self-Assessment

2. Self-Monitoring, and

3. Self-Reinforcement

**Self-Assessment** (SA) refers to students systematically examining their own behavior and determining whether or not they have performed a specific behavior or class of behaviors. The students behave and then evaluate their behavior. An example of SA might be a student who has been taught to systematically evaluate how "on-task" he or she was during reading class by rating on-task behavior using a scale of one to five.

Certainly we all evaluate our behavior regularly. Each time you perform a task, you tell yourself your performance was adequate or not. Most children evaluate themselves on the basis of "self-evaluation standards" acquired from "significant others" in their environment (Bandura, 1977). Children's parents, in particular, provide them with standards on which to evaluate their behavior in various situations. However, for numerous reasons, some children fail to acquire clear self-evaluation standards, or standards they can use in very specific situations, In such cases, it is necessary to teach SA skills directly.

A number of studies have examined the efficacy of various SA methods. Blackwood (1970) and Kaufman and O'Leary (1972), for example, found that SA methods can be used to reduce disruptive behavior. Bornstein and Quevillon (1976) found that they can be used to increase on-task behavior.

**Self-Monitoring** (SM) refers to a procedure wherein students systematically monitor and record their performance of certain behaviors, keeping a record of how often and to what extent they engage in some activity.

The very act of monitoring one's actions has been found to have an effect on the behavior being monitored (Workman & Hector, 1978). For example, if a student monitors a behavior that is strongly encouraged in the classroom, that behavior will increase. If the student monitors a behavior that is strongly discouraged, the behavior will decrease. Recent research has shown that SM can be used to increase academic achievement (Piersel & Kratochwill, 1979) and reduce disruptive behavior (Moletzky, 1974).

**Self-Reinforcement** (SR) refers to students giving themselves reinforcers when they behave appropriately. Whenever a teacher rewards a student for behaving appropriately, the student's appropriate behavior will occur more often. This fact is based on the well-known **principle of positive reinforcement** (Kazdin, 1980). SR is also based on the principle of positive reinforcement. Whenever a student reinforces himself for an appropriate behavior, that behavior will begin to occur more often.

More classroom research has been conducted on SR than any other BSC procedure (Workman & Hector, 1978). The research has demonstrated that SR is highly effective in increasing students' on-task behavior (Glynn, et al., 1973), enhancing academic achievement (Humphrey & Karoly, 1978), and reducing disruptive behavior (Bolstad & Johnson, 1972). Quite clearly, SR represents one of the most effective and versatile components of BSC.


## SUMMARY

In this chapter, we've examined the use of BSC as an important phase in the behavior change process and explored the rationale for using BSC with students in classroom settings. BSC (1) allows students to manage their own behavior in the absence of the teacher and other supporting adults, (2) teaches students to take responsibility for their own behavior, and (3) enhances the maintenance and generalization of Phase I behavior modification programs.

BSC procedures were shown to be effective in changing three types of student behaviors critical to the learning process: (1) on-task behavior, (2) academic product behavior, and (3) disruptive behavior.

Finally, we briefly examined the basic components of BSC programs: Self-Assessment, Self-Monitoring, and Self-Reinforcement. In subsequent chapters, we'll discuss the techniques of BSC in greater detail and you will learn to use them in your classroom.

# II

# Principles and Techniques of Behavioral Self-Control (BSC)

This chapter explores the basic principles of BSC and techniques derived from these principles. Self-Assessment (SA), Self-Monitoring (SM), and Self-Reinforcement (SR) yield a number of different techniques you can teach your students to use. We'll discuss each of these and describe some of the research which supports their use in classrooms.

## SELF-ASSESSMENT (SA)

As you learned in the previous chapter, Self-Assessment (SA) refers to students assessing or evaluating their behavior so as to improve it. Three SA techniques can be used in classrooms: Self-Ratings, Self-Instruction Training, and Verbal Mediation Training.

### Self-Ratings

This technique involves students being taught to rate their behavior according to some rating scale. The scale provides the students with an objective standard on which to evaluate their behavior. For example, students might be taught to rate their on-task behavior during a one-hour period each day, using a scale of zero to five. They were trained to give themselves a zero if they weren't on-task at all during the period; a five if they were on-task almost constantly; and numbers between zero and five for the degrees in between.

Kaufman and O'Leary (1972) examined the effects of Self-Ratings using a class of psychiatric school students. The students were taught to rate themselves on the basis of how well they followed classroom rules. The result was a dramatic decrease in the students' disruptive behavior. More importantly, the Self-Rating procedure proved just as effective as a Phase I token reinforcement procedure which preceded it!

### Self-Instruction Training

This involves teaching students to cue themselves verbally to perform tasks in a particular manner and then to provide themselves with verbal feedback about the adequacy of their performance (Meichenbaum & Goodman, 1971). In other words, it teaches students to talk to themselves appropriately, providing them with a set of standards on which to assess their performance and an effective means of verbally guiding their own behavior.

Although we might not like to admit it and don't do it in public, we all talk to ourselves almost all the time. We tell ourselves what to do to solve certain problems and whether or not our performance was "up to par." Interestingly, recent research

(Kendall, 1977) has indicated that children with various types of school problems are not very skillful in talking to themselves. These children appear to lack the ability to guide their own behavior verbally and evaluate the adequacy of their own performance. Self-Instruction Training provides a quick and effective means of remediating this problem. In a study with several "overactive" and "impulsive" pre-school children, Bornstein and Quevillon (1976) evaluated the effects of Self-Instruction Training. During a single two hour training period, the children were taught to ask themselves questions about tasks, correct themselves when they erred, and praise themselves for correct performance. Prior to the training, the students were on-task (following directions, paying attention) only about 11% of the time they were observed. After only one two-hour session, the students were on-task about 80% of the time. This dramatic increase in on-task behavior was maintained during a 23-week follow up period.

## Verbal Mediation Training

Early in the 1970s, Blackwood (1970) developed a procedure highly similar to Self-Instruction Training which he called Verbal Mediation Training. It involves having students copy essays which teach them to assess their own behavior. It is based on the idea that having students write essays answering questions about their behavior will encourage them to think (i.e., talk to themselves) about what behaviors are required by classroom rules as well as about the consequences of various appropriate and inappropriate behaviors. In this way, the students learn to assess their behavior in relation to classroom rules, and thereby control their own behavior.

In order to evaluate the effects of this approach, Blackwood (1970) had 12 highly disruptive eighth and ninth grade students write two different types of essays. A student who engaged in disruptive behavior was required to copy an essay as "punishment" each time such behavior occurred. One group of six students copied an essay about a topic unrelated to their behavior. The other six students, however, copied an essay which specifically answered questions about the type of disruptive behavior which led to their punishment. After 15 days, the essay related to the behavior reduced the students' average rate of disruptive behavior from about one disruptive incident per 10-minute period to essentially zero disruptive incidents per class session. The unrelated essay resulted in essentially no changes in student behavior.

Perhaps the most important aspect of the Blackwood (1970) study involves the fact that prior to the essays, all twelve students had been exposed to a Phase I behavior modification program. Although this program reduced disruptive behavior, the Verbal Mediation Training procedure reduced disruptive behavior even further, enhancing the effectiveness of the Phase I behavior modification program.

## SELF-MONITORING (SM)

You remember that Self-Monitoring (SM) is a procedure in which students monitor and record their performance of a given behavior or class of behaviors. With SM, students are taught to keep a record of how often or to what extent they engage in some activity. The act of monitoring actions has been found to have an effect on the behavior being monitored. Behaviors that the teacher strongly encourages are increased by self-monitoring. Conversely, behaviors that are discouraged will decrease.

Two types of SM procedures have been found to be highly effective in improving students' behavior: Frequency Self-Monitoring and Interval Self-Monitoring.

### Frequency Self-Monitoring

This involves teaching a student to monitor and record the number of times a behavior occurs. It is based on the use of **frequency count observations** (Kazdin, 1980) wherein someone records each occurrence of a student's behavior. With Frequency Self-Monitoring the students monitor their own behavior, recording each occurrence of the behavior to be changed.

Piersel and Kratochwill (1979) have presented an excellent set of studies evaluating the effects of Frequency Self-Monitoring on student achievement. In one study, a second grade student was taught to monitor and record, on paper, the number of language arts problems she correctly completed each day. Before the program, the student correctly completed about 30% of her language problems, on the average. When she started using the simple SM procedure, her performance improve dramatically, to about 95% correct. More importantly, the effect of the program lasted for the duration of the study—fifty-eight days.

In another study, Piersel and Kratochwill (1979) taught a middle school student to monitor and record his completion of language and math units in a packaged curricular program. Prior to learning the Frequency Self-Monitoring technique, the student had completed two language and zero math assignments in a six-week period. After being taught their technique, the student successfully completed seventeen language units within four weeks and ten math units within two and one-half weeks, a substantial improvement.

In the above studies, Frequency Self-Monitoring was used to increase desirable student behaviors. Being extremely versatile, however, it can also be used to decrease undesirable behaviors. Moletzky (1974) reported a number of studies which illustrate this use. In one of these, a nine year old who raised his hand furiously even when he couldn't correctly respond to the teacher's questions was taught to monitor his disruptive behavior with a wrist counter (see Chapter III). The hand raising decreased to zero. After about six weeks, the procedure was terminated, but the student's disruptive hand raising stayed at zero throughout a six-month follow-up period!

Moletzky's (1974) second case study focused on an eleven year-old student who got out of her seat excessively. This child was also taught to monitor her disruptive behavior with a wrist counter. As with the previous case, Frequency Self-Monitoring resulted in a dramatic decrease in disruptive behavior from twenty-three disruptive incidents per day to two per day. Equally important is the fact that following the removal of the procedure, the student's disruptions remained at an acceptably low rate throughout a six-month follow-up period.

### Interval Self-Monitoring

This involves teaching a student to monitor his behavior and record the presence of absence of a particular behavior during a given interval of time. It is based on **interval observation** procedures (Wahler, House, & Stambaugh, 1976), in which an observer periodically observes a student (every 10 or 15 seconds) and makes a record of what behaviors occurred during each time interval. In

Interval Self-Monitoring, the student rather than an observer makes the observations.

The effectiveness of this SM technique has been demonstrated in a recent study conducted by Workman, Helton, and Watson (1982). These researchers taught a preschool child to monitor his behavior and record whether or not he was on-task during assignments. The student placed a mark on a sheet of paper if, and only if, he had been on-task whenever a signal was emitted by a kitchen timer. The timer went off every five minutes. Use of Interval Self-Monitoring resulted in raising the student's average rate of on-task behavior from 37% (observed during an eight day period prior to the program) to approximately 64%. Also, the improvement generalized to another behavior. The student began complying with approximately 30% more teacher instructions than he did before the Interval Self-Monitoring was implemented.

So far, you have seen studies demonstrating that SM can be used to increase some behaviors and decrease others. "How is this possible?" you might ask. "How can a single procedure result in totally opposite effects on different behaviors?" And, furthermore, "How do you know whether SM will increase or decrease a student's behavior? What is there to prevent SM from decreasing a desirable behavior or increasing an undesirable behavior?"

The answer to these questions lies in the specific situation in which a given behavior occurs. As Workman and Hector (1978) have suggested, those behaviors that lead to positive outcomes or rewards are likely to be increased with SM, whereas those with negative outcomes are likely to be decreased. As was previously stated, those behaviors that you strongly encourage in your class, like completing assignments, will most likely increase with SM. Those that you strongly discourage, like disruptions, will most likely decrease. It appears that SM magnifies whatever outcomes a student's behavior naturally produces in your class, whether encouragement or discouragement.

One possible reason for the magnification effect is that SM may increase students' awareness of what's going on around them. If there is a strong natural relationship between completing assignments and positive events such as being praised, gaining status, etc., and the students become more aware of this relationship, then it would be reasonable to assume that they would increase their rate of assignment completion in order to obtain more praise and status. On the other hand, if students become more aware of a strong natural relationship between a behavior and negative events, like criticism, you would expect that the student would engage in that behavior less often.

Almost all teachers have encountered students with whom normal amounts of encouragement or discouragement have little or no effect. Our analysis of the effects of SM suggest that you may be able to reach such students by magnifying encouragement or discouragement with SM. Furthermore, it also suggests that you can enhance the effects of your ordinary praise or reprimands.

You might also ask whether SM can be used with any but the brightest students. After all, SM appears to involve a relatively complex skill requiring a high degree of concentration and intelligence. The clearest response to this concern is contained in a study conducted by Litrownik, Freitas, and Franzini (1978). These researchers successfully taught SM procedures to children with IQs between 30 and 50, the Trainable Mentally Retarded. In another study, Mahoney and Mahoney (1976) successfully taught SM skills to children with IQs of 50 to 70, the Educable Mentally Retarded. Studies such as these rather clearly indicate that SM can be used with almost any student attending school.

## SELF-REINFORCEMENT (SR)

As you remember from the previous chapter, Self-Reinforcement (SR) involves teaching students to reinforce or reward themselves for appropriate classroom behaviors. Like teacher reinforcement, student SR increases those behaviors that are reinforced. Two SR methods have been successfully used in classroom situations: Overt Self-Reinforcement and Covert Positive Reinforcement.

### Overt Self-Reinforcement

In this technique, students administer overt (observable and tangible) reinforcers to themselves after they engage in certain appropriate behaviors. A number of studies have shown that a variety of classroom behaviors can be strengthened through Overt Self-Reinforcement and that the technique can be taught to students of practically all ages (Workman & Hector, 1978).

Using a whole classroom of second grade students, Glynn, Thomas, and Shee (1973) examined the effects of Overt Self-Reinforcement on on-task behavior. The students were taught to notice whether they were on-task when a signal was emitted by a tape recorder. Students who were on-task rewarded themselves with one point. The points could be exchanged for extra recess time. During a baseline condition in which no behavior change procedure was in effect, the average student in the class was on-task only 58% of the time. During periods when OSR was used, the average student was on-task 93% of the time!

Prior to the Overt Self-Reinforcement program, the teacher used a Phase I reward system in which students received tokens when they were on-task. This resulted in an on-task rate of 81%. Although 81% represents a dramatic increase from the baseline level, the Overt Self-Reinforcement program resulted in even higher levels of on-task behavior. It should also be noted that when the token rewards were removed, the on-task behavior decreased to an average of 55%, leaving the students back where they started. When the Overt Self-Reinforcement procedure was removed, the students' on-task behavior dropped to 75%, a figure still substantially higher than the baseline period! This suggests that the program is internalized by the students, allowing for maintenance of effects. The technique may become a normal feature of the students' behavior, such that they will naturally reward themselves (with positive self-talk, for example) when they perform well.

In another study, Humphrey and Karoly (1978) examined the effects of Overt Self-Reinforcers on the reading performance of a group of second grade students. The students were taught to reward themselves with colored plastic chips when they appropriately completed daily reading assignments in the form of reading passages and answering questions. This procedure increased the number of daily assignments completed by each student from an average of less than two (during a baseline period) to an average of four. The students' average percentage of correct responses on the assignments was initially high and did not change during the program. Overt Self-Reinforcement literally doubled the students' rate of assignment completion while maintaining accuracy!

The same study by Humphrey and Karoly (1978) also examined the effects of a self-punishment procedure on reading behavior, in which the students removed tokens from their cups (a response cost technique) for incorrect answers. Although the procedure increased the students' rates of assignment completion, it was concluded that self-punishment was not as effective as SR, a result clearly in line with the general preference for positive behavior change techniques (Clarizio, 1980).

Using 128 ninth grade students, Glynn (1970) examined the effect of Overt Self-Reinforcement on the accuracy of responses to daily quizzes in history and geography classes. The students were taught to reward themselves with one token for each set of four correct answers. The results indicated that the procedure resulted in significant increases in the number of items each student answered correctly on quizzes. Overt Self-Reinforcement can be used not only to increase productivity, but also to increase the quality of students' work!!

In the preceding studies, the goal was to increase some desirable classroom behavior. Overt Self-Reinforcement can also be used to decrease undesirable behaviors by teaching students to reward themselves for low rates of unwanted behaviors. For example, Bolstad and Johnson (1972) examined the effects of OSR and Phase I token reinforcement on disruptive behaviors, such as being out of seat, and hitting and talking out, of a group of first and second grade students. Following a brief Phase I token program where the teacher rewarded all students for low rates of disruption, one group of students was taught to give themselves points for not exceeding a certain number of disruptive behaviors each day. The other students continued to be rewarded by the teacher for low rates of disruptive behavior. The results of the study indicated that both Overt Self-Reinforcement and traditional teacher reinforcement were effective in reducing disruptive behavior. However, the authors of the study concluded that the SR program was slightly more effective than the traditional token program! Since the Overt Self-Reinforcement program followed the Phase I program, it apparently can be used to enhance the effectiveness of more traditional, Phase I, procedures.

All the studies described in this section suggest that Overt Self-Reinforcement is equally as effective as traditional Phase I behavior modification programs in improving student performance. Moreover, this appears to be true with a variety of classroom-relevant performance areas, including on-task behavior, assignment completion, accuracy of academic responses, and disruptive behavior.

## Covert Positive Reinforcement

Like the previous program, this involves teaching students to reward themselves for appropriate behavior; however, the rewards are not tangible and observable. In Covert Positive Reinforcement, students are taught to imagine themselves engaging in appropriate behaviors and then imagine themselves receiving some highly valued reward. The teacher usually leads students in doing this five to ten times each day. That is, students, are instructed to imagine (1) the behavior to be improved and (2) a highly reinforcing event, five to ten times each day.

Several studies have shown that the program is effective in improving students' behavior. For example, Workman and Dickinson (1979) trained a third grade student to imagine himself being on-task (working in his seat quietly) and then imagine himself receiving one of several highly valued rewards. After only several days, this procedure reduced the student's off-task behaviors, being out-of seat and talking out, by an average of 42%.

## EXPERIENCE WITH PHASE I BEHAVIOR MODIFICATION PROGRAMS

As you probably noted, some of the studies discussed in this chapter exposed students to Phase I behavior modification programs prior to teaching BSC skills. Others simply skipped Phase I and taught BSC skills directly. Workman and Hector (1978) suggested that, in some cases, prior exposure to systematic external reinforcement might enhance the effectiveness of BSC. Some researchers, for example Glynn (1970), have suggested that students who have not been previously exposed to well-structured Phase I environments, either at home or school, might learn BSC skills less readily than other students.

Walker's (1979) model conceptualizes BSC as the second step in the behavior change process, following external teacher reinforcement. However, there is presently no conclusive evidence that some students need prior experience with systematic external reinforcement in order to learn BSC. In fact, a number of the studies described in this chapter (Humphrey & Karoly, 1978; Glynn, 1970; Bornstein & Quevillon, 1976; Moletzky, 1974) obtained excellent effects with BSC without the use of prior reinforcement programs. This suggests that you might teach BSC to your students without first using a Phase I program. However, if you feel that many of the students in your class are from environments lacking structure, you should consider exposing them to external reinforcement prior to BSC. For example, you might set up an external token reinforcement program where you reinforce students for appropriate behavior, use it for only a brief period (two to five days), and then shift to the use of a BSC procedure.


## ACCURACY OF STUDENTS' SELF-MONITORING AND SELF-REINFORCEMENT

Some of you may be wondering just how accurate are students' recordings of their own behavior. You may also be concerned that some students might cheat and give themselves more points or tokens than they deserve. Surprising to some, most BSC programs are not plagued by accuracy or cheating problems (Workman & Hector, 1978). If the teacher clearly (verbally) encourages accuracy, most students are able to accurately monitor their own behavior and do not give themselves more points or tokens than earned.

If, for some reason, you find that some of your students cannot accurately record or reward themselves, there are two methods for solving this problem. The first involves reinforcing students for accuracy. In the Bolstad and Johnson (1972) study, the classroom teacher briefly rewarded students with points for having self-monitored data which matched (within reasonable limits) data she obtained. In the second method, developed by Hundert and Bastone (1978), the teacher verbally prohibits dishonesty and then tells the students that their work or records will be checked. Furthermore, the teacher indicates that "action" will be taken if cheating occurs. In reality, the teacher does not check the students' work, since it would be rather time consuming. Hundert and Bastone (1978) found that this procedure dramatically reduced the inaccurate recording of several students who were prone toward "overestimating" their correct answers on problems, in order to receive maximum rewards. Apparently, the mere threat of punishment and the illusion of surveillance creates an atmosphere that inhibits inaccurate self-recording.

## SUMMARY

In this chapter we have explored a variety of BSC techniques which can be used in the classroom. Extensive research indicates that these procedures are highly effective in improving students' behavior. For your convenience we have included an appendix which provides a glossary of all the techniques discussed in this chapter and the remainder of the book.

# III

# Self-Assessment (SA)

This chapter focuses on practical procedures for implementing SA systems in the classroom, including Self-Ratings, Self-Instruction Training, and Verbal Mediation Training. You will be presented with step-by-step methods for implementing these procedures in order to change various classroom behaviors. Also, we'll take a look at a number of various classroom case studies which exemplify the use of BSC in classroom settings.

## SELF-RATINGS

As with any BSC system, your first step is to decide what specific student behavior you want to change and in what situation you want to change it. In other words, you must **select a target behavior** and decide where you want this behavior to occur or not occur. Although your students may have several behaviors you want to change, you should attempt to teach your students to deal with only one behavior at a time.

Trying to change too many behaviors simultaneously only serves to confuse students and lowers the probability of success. If you start out trying to change a single behavior, you increase your chances for success. After you have succeeded in changing one behavior, you can then attempt to change others.

After you have selected a target behavior, the next step is to **devise a rating system.** The rating system will allow your students to have a "yardstick" by which to assess the appropriateness of their behavior. The rating system should generally range from either zero to five or zero to two. With younger children a zero to two scale is preferable since it will require less complex discriminations. You should define for your students, as clearly and objectively as possible, each point on the rating scale. For example, suppose your target behavior is to be on-task during math class. You would first tell your student what on-task means (e.g., paying attention and doing assigned work in one's seat). You would then define the scale to the students, for example, tell them that "you give yourself a zero if you weren't on-task very much at all, a one if you were on-task but not all of the time, and a two if you were on-task all of the time."

After devising a scale, your next step is to **determine the interval** during which daily self-ratings will take place. In other words, you decide whether you want your students to rate themselves after each period of five minutes, fifteen minutes, thirty minutes, one hour, two hours, or one day. In general, the shorter the interval the better, since the students will more accurately remember recent behavior. However, manageability should also be considered. Longer intervals are usually more manageable than shorter ones. If you decide on a fifteen-minute interval, you would briefly stop class every fifteen minutes and ask your class to rate themselves. Younger children, especially, need to be periodically reminded of both the definition of the target behavior and the meaning of each number of the scale.

Once you have chosen an interval, you may want to vary it from time to time. For example, with a fifteen-minute interval, you might mostly use fifteen-minute intervals, but occasionally use fourteen, eighteen, or twelve minutes. This will keep the students from anticipating the forthcoming rating time and improving their behavior near that point. Since they will not know exactly when they will rate themselves, varying the intervals will encourage them to "spread out" their good behavior.

You might also progressively increase your interval as the students' behavior improves. For example, you might start out using a five-minute interval. After several days, you notice that the students' behavior has improved, as indicated by your informal observations and the fact that most students are getting two's on a scale of zero to two on every interval. At this point, you might increase the interval to fifteen minutes, and later, as the students continue to improve, to thirty minutes or one hour.

After you have chosen an initial rating interval, your next and final step before implementing the Self-Rating system is to **decide on the mechanics** of the system. In other words, you must determine precisely how the students will carry out the rating procedure. Will they simply place the numeral 0, 1, or 2 on the top of any sheet of paper? Or will they use a uniform recording system? Although you should let creativity be your guide, a rating sheet taped to the students' desks is more likely to survive the bustle of the classroom than is an unattached sheet of paper. Examples of rating forms that can be attached to each student's desk are found in Figures 4 and 5.

Below are the steps in setting up a Self-Assessment program.

1. **Select the Target Behavior.** Determine exactly what student behavior you want to change. Tell your students exactly what this behavior involves.

2. **Devise a Rating System.** Decide how you want your students to rate their performance of the Target Behavior. Spell out what level of performance is required for each rating.

3. **Determine the Rating System Interval.** Choose the time period you want your students to rate themselves.

4. **Design the Mechanics of the System.** Design a form on which your students can rate themselves.

5. **Implement the System.** Explain the system, telling your students why you want them to rate themselves, and have them begin doing so.

**Figure 4**
**Sample Self-Rating Form #1**

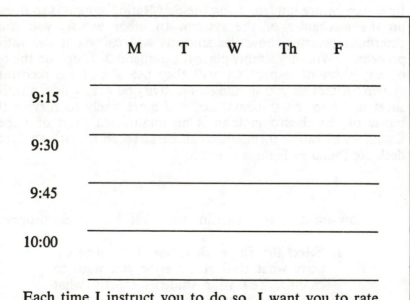

|  | M | T | W | Th | F |
|---|---|---|---|---|---|
| 9:15 | | | | | |
| 9:30 | | | | | |
| 9:45 | | | | | |
| 10:00 | | | | | |

Each time I instruct you to do so, I want you to rate yourself on how well you've been paying attention. Give yourself a "0" if you haven't been paying attention very well at all, a "1" if you've been paying attention fairly well, and a "2" if you've really been paying attention extremely well.

## Figure 5
## Sample Self-Rating Form #2

|         | M | T | W | Th | F |
|---------|---|---|---|----|---|
| 10:15   |   |   |   |    |   |
| 10:30   |   |   |   |    |   |
| 10:45   |   |   |   |    |   |
| 11:00   |   |   |   |    |   |

Each time I give you the signal, I want you to rate yourself on how much time you've been participating in our group discussion. Give yourself a "0" if you haven't been participating at all, a "1" if you've participated a little, and a "2" if you've participated a great deal.

Let's review the steps in the use of Self-Ratings with an example from an actual case study. This study was conducted in Ms. Foster's fourth grade class. The procedures focused on her students' math class performance.

1. **Select the Target Behavior.** Ms. Foster decided that her students were not working as hard as they should during math class. It took place right after gym and too many of the students seemed more interested in

daydreaming and staring out the window than learning math. Ms. Foster, therefore, decided that she would use BSC to increase the students' **on-task behavior.** She defined on-task behavior as working on math problems, reading instructions from the math book, or looking at and listening to her while she demonstrated a problem on the board.

2. **Devise a Rating System.** Ms. Foster decided to use a zero-to-two rating system, one that all students in her class would clearly understand. With this system, students gave themselves a "0" if they had not been on-task at all, a "1" if they had been on-task part but not most of the time, and a "2" if they had been on-task most of the time.

3. **Determine the Rating System Interval.** Since Ms. Foster had a large number of students in her class, many requiring individual attention, she decided that a five- or ten-minute interval would be cumbersome, so she chose a twenty-minute interval. In order to avoid having to looking at her watch frequently, Ms. Foster brought a kitchen timer from home and set it to ring every twenty minutes (three times during the math class).

4. **Design the Mechanics of the Rating System.** Ms. Foster developed a rating sheet that had the numerals 0, 1, and 2 listed three times under each day, as in the sample

| M | T | W | Th | F |
|---|---|---|----|---|
| 0 1 2 | 0 1 2 | 0 1 2 | 0 1 2 | 0 1 2 |
| 0 1 2 | 0 1 2 | 0 1 2 | 0 1 2 | 0 1 2 |
| 0 1 2 | 0 1 2 | 0 1 2 | 0 1 2 | 0 1 2 |

The students taped a rating sheet to their desks. Each time the timer's bell rang, Ms. Foster instructed the students to circle the appropriate number, depending upon their on-task behavior since the start of class or the last time the bell rang.

5. **Implement the System.** After the first four steps were completed, Ms. Foster implemented the Self-Rating program. The first day she told the students to try to get as many "2s" as possible, because the names of students with all "2s" would be placed under a "class hero" section of the blackboard each day. This procedure served to link SA success with peer status. In other words, self-control skill was tied to some important social status reinforcers.

In addition to the above procedures, Ms. Foster told the students she would be observing them to insure accuracy and that "cheating" would be punished by loss of recess for the day.

The results of Ms. Foster's program were quite impressive. After approximately three weeks, over 95% of her students were receiving at least three "2s" each day. Also, she reported that the average student's math performance had improved dramatically. The effects that the Self-Rating program had on math performance are shown in Figure 6.

## Figure 6
## Effects of Self-Rating Program on Math Performance

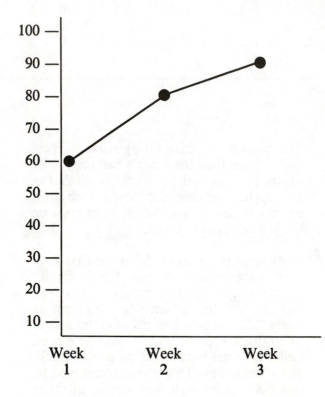

Average number of correct problems
in daily math quizzes

The average student in Ms. Foster's class went from approximately 60% of math quiz items correct during the first week of
self-ratings to approximately 90% of items correct during the
third week. It seems reasonable to assume that these academic
improvements were, at least in part, related to improvements in
the students' on-task behavior during math.

## SELF-INSTRUCTION TRAINING

Unlike almost all of the other BSC procedures discussed in this book, Self-Instruction Training is used only to change a specific class of student behaviors. While the other BSC techniques can be adapted for use in changing most any classroom behavior, Self-Instruction Training is used to **reduce impulsive/disruptive behaviors** and **increase on-task behavior.** It is used with children who have trouble paying attention and following directions (either in terms of specific school tasks or general requests) and those who tend to disruptively "jump" from one activity to another. The specific procedures discussed here are most suitable for younger, early elementary, students.

Although most research (e.g., Bornstein & Quevillon, 1976) uses individual sessions, Self-Instruction Training can also be carried out with small groups of students. We will confine our discussion to the group approach, since it is most feasible for the majority of school settings.

A Self-Instruction Training group can consist of up to three or four students. Classroom teachers will have to divide the class into five or six small groups, so that all students can participate. The training takes a total of about two hours. You could teach the procedure to each group for about one hour a day for three days, or for about thirty minutes a day for six days. With a relatively large group, the training time could be increased to four or five hours so that each child receives individual attention.

In terms of logistics, the best method is to have those students not being trained engage in a group or individual task that will occupy them for the training period. Although you can work with each group in one corner of your classroom, you might want to appoint a student monitor to reduce the possibility of distractions. If, for some reason, you find it inconvenient to have the two training sessions during class time, you might try using recess periods.

Now, let's take a close look at the Self-Instruction Training procedures developed by Bornstein and Quevillon (1976). The following six-step program moves from speaking aloud to thinking.

> 1. Model a classroom task while repeating
>    aloud the steps in completing the task.

2. Have your students complete the task while you verbalize aloud.

3. Have your students complete the task while they verbalize aloud.

4. Have your students complete the task while whispering.

5. Have each student complete the task while making lip movements.

6. Have each student complete the task while thinking about the steps in the task.

Before beginning, select three or four classroom tasks to use in the Self-Instruction Training. Each of the six steps should be completed with all tasks before proceeding to the next task. The tasks should be common classroom activities which involve a major visual component, so the students can clearly see the steps necessary to complete the tasks. Although the tasks you use will depend upon what you have your students do in class, examples might include drawing a picture of a specific object, writing answers to questions from a reading passage, writing or printing sentences, matching geometric forms, and working specific types of math problems on paper.

Step 1 involves modeling or demonstrating a classroom task to the group saying the steps involved out loud. Don't worry about talking out loud to yourself. Your students will see it as completely natural since you'll be describing the task being modelled.

While modelling the task, you must verbalize out loud four types of statements: (1) questions about task requirements: "What am I supposed to do?"; (2) answers to such questions: ("That's right, I'm supposed to draw lines to show which two pictures are alike."; (3) self-instructions that serve as guides for completing the task: "Alright, first I go to the next picture, then I draw a line from that picture to the one that looks like it . . ."; and (4) self-reinforcement statements: "That's right, that line looks really good; I'm doing a great job!" In addition, you should occasionally make an intentional error and correct it immediately. This will serve to model being alert to possible errors and ways to correct them immediately.

In order for Self-Instruction Training to be effective, the students must pay close attention to your modelling and follow the instructions in the first and subsequent steps. If the students have trouble attending or complying with instructions, use the following procedure: (1) repeat instructions to "watch what I do and listen to what I say," and (2) when each child is paying attention, give the child a raisin, a piece of candy, or a token which is exchangeable for some reward. This will serve to "shape up" tne students' attending and compliance initially, but should be stopped as soon as the students can complete the tasks. You should spend about twenty to thirty minutes on this and each of the other six steps in SIT.

Step 2 involves instructing the students to complete the task, while you verbalize the four statements out loud. You should encourage all of the students in the group to work simultaneously on the task and listen to your statements. You can either have all the students work on each step at the same time, or you can let them take turns performing and watching. Make sure that you encourage the students to try to match, with their task performances, what you are verbalizing. Your statements are guiding the rate they perform the tasks.

Step 3 involves having each student (in turn or simultaneously) perform the task while saying the four statements out loud. While each student does this, you must whisper the statements loud enough that the students can hear you. Whispering serves as a "prompt" for the students' correctly verbalizing the statements.

Step 4 involves having each student perform the task while softly whispering the four statements. As the student is doing this, you prompt the student by making lip movements of the four statements. What is happening here is that you're fading (slowly removing) the prompts for appropriate "self-talk," while the student is internalizing the statements. In other words, the students are learning to talk to themselves in a way that will guide them to stay on task.

Step 5 entails each student performing the task while making the lip movements for the four statements. You simply watch and praise appropriate task performance.

Step 6 involves having each student perform the task while thinking the four statements. By now, you have completely removed the prompts and the student has completely internalized the self-instructions. This should result in an increased ability to stay on-task and, therefore, appropriately complete assignments.

Let's look at a case study demonstrating the use of Self-Instruction Training, which took place in a first grade class in a suburban school. Mr. Thompson's class included about seven youngsters who had serious difficulty staying on task during reading. His diagnostic assessments of their reading skills had shown that all the children possessed the basic skills necessary to successfully attack tasks. So, after consulting with the author of this book, Mr. Thompson decided to implement a Self-Instruction Training program.

Mr. Thompson included four of the problem students in one group and three in another. He conducted one two-hour session with each group, while his aide managed the classroom. In these sessions, the students learned to verbally guide their own performance on tasks involving matching pictures and words. Following the training, Mr. Thompson observed a dramatic improvement in the students' behavior. These results are shown in Figure 7.

**Figure 7**
**Effects of Self-Instruction Training (SIT)**

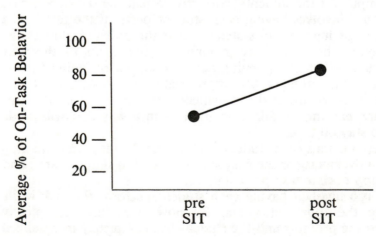

The results in Figure 7 are based Mr. Thompson's systematic observations of all seven students' behavior the day before and the day after the training. Prior to the training, the average student was on task during reading only about 52% of the time; afterwards, on-task behavior increased to approximately 83%. In addition, Mr. Thompson reported that the students' disruptive behaviors decreased dramatically.

## VERBAL MEDIATION TRAINING

Although Blackwoods' (1970) Verbal Mediation Training is somewhat similar to Self-Instruction Training in intent, it is substantially easier to implement. Also, whereas Self-Instruction Training is used with elementary age students, Verbal Mediation Training is used with older students, able to print or write, who have trouble following various rules.

The training consists of having students copy essays as a consequence of misbehavior. Each time a student misbehaves, a copy of the appropriate essay is dropped on his or her desk. Essays are designed for each misbehavior the teacher wants to reduce: for example, there is one for out-of-seat behavior, one for talking out, one for hitting others, etc.

Prior to the implementation of the program, you inform the students that when they receive an essay, you want them to make two copies of the essay by the next morning. If a student does not complain when receiving an essay and engages in no other misbehaviors during the period, the assignment is reduced to only one essay. Students who do not submit the required number of essays the following morning will receive after-school detention when the essay is to be copied.

The teacher must prepare different essays for each type of inappropriate behavior over which the students will learn self-control. The essays are written at the appropriate vocabulary level and clearly refer to the behavior in question. Each essay contains four questions and answers: (1) "What did I do wrong?"; (2) "What is wrong with that behavior?"; (3) "What should I have been doing instead?"; and (4) "Why should I have been doing _____ (the named behavior)?" After each question is a paragraph which vividly provides an answer.

Here is a case study showing the use of an essay about talking inappropriately during class. This essay was used by Ms. James, a junior high school math teacher with whom the author recently worked to reduce this behavior. The Verbal Mediation Training essay consisted of the following four questions:

1. **What did I do wrong?** I was talking without permission while Ms. James was teaching class.

2. **What is wrong with talking without permission?** Talking without permission keeps myself and other students from hearing the teacher, and I will miss out on something that might be on a test. If I miss out on one part of the class, I won't understand the rest, and I will become bored. If I talk without permission, I will have to write an essay like this or I will have to stay after school.

3. **What should I have been doing instead of talking?** Instead of talking, I should have been listening to Ms. James and following the lesson. If I wanted to say something I should have raised my hand for permission.

4. **Why should I have been listening and following the lesson?** I should have been listening and following the lesson so I would understand it and make a good grade on the test. I should have raised my hand for permission to speak so as not to disrupt the class. If I had obtained permission, I could have spoken without getting in trouble.

The results of Ms. James' Verbal Mediation Training program are shown in Figure 8.

## Figure 8
## Effects of Verbal Mediation Training Program (VMT)

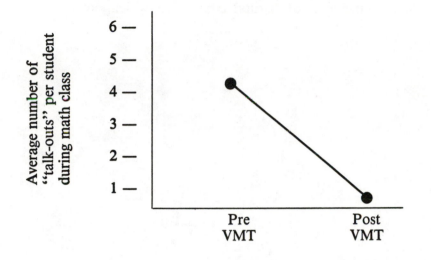

These results are based on the author's observations in Ms. James' classroom before and after the training program.

After Ms. James used the talking out essay for about two weeks, the level of inappropriate talking in her eighth grade class was reduced from an average of about four per student to almost zero! Evidently, the students had learned to talk to themselves in such a manner as to inhibit talking-out. In other words, the students had acquired a BSC skill which reduced disruptive behavior.

## SUMMARY

In this chapter, we've examined three self-assessment procedures which can be taught to students: Self-Ratings, Self-Instruction

Training, and Verbal Mediation Training. Self-Ratings can be used with students of most any age range to improve a wide variety of behaviors. Self-Instruction Training is used primarily with early elementary students to increase on-task behavior and reduce disruptiveness. Verbal Mediation Training can be used with middle elementary, junior high, and high school students to reduce the incidence of disruptive behaviors which violate rules.

# IV

# Self-Monitoring (SM)

As you saw in Chapter II, students can learn to monitor their own behavior and thereby attain self-control. The very act of monitoring behavior increases a student's on-going awareness of behavior. If a behavior is strongly encouraged in the classroom, increased student awareness of its occurrence will tend to result in an increase in the rate of that behavior, in other words, the behavior will occur more often. Conversely, if a behavior is strongly discouraged in the classroom, increased student awareness will tend to decrease that behavior. In Chapter IV, we will examine two Self-Monitoring methods which can be taught to students: Frequency Self-Monitoring and Interval Self-Monitoring.

## FREQUENCY SELF-MONITORING

In this method, the student records each behavior as it occurs, eventually obtaining a "count," sometimes called a frequency count, which represents the total number of times a behavior occurred on a given day. Behaviors counted by students could include the number of times each day they talk out without permission, get out of their seats without permission, or engage in inappropriate noise-making activities. Desirable behaviors can also be counted, such as the number of math or reading problems completed each day, the number of such problems completed correctly, and the number of paragraphs read during seatwork periods. As these examples suggest, Frequency Self-Monitoring is used to record discrete behaviors. That is, the behaviors have a clearly definable beginning and end, and they tend to occur, or should occur, quickly and often.

Students can be taught to make frequency counts of their behavior by using paper and pencil or mechanical recording devices. A sheet of paper or an index card taped to the student's desk can serve as a pencil and paper device. A wrist "golf-counter," available inexpensively at most sporting goods stores, can serve as a mechanical device. The author strongly recommends paper and pencil devices; they are simple to use and inexpensive. Also, they provide students with an immediate visual record of progress, which tends to motivate students by providing success feedback. Students need only glance at their recording sheets to see clear-cut improvement and evidence of personal success.

Some examples of paper and pencil devices for Frequency Self-Monitoring are shown in Figures 9, 10, and 11.

In order to implement a Frequency Self-Monitoring procedure in the classroom using paper and pencil devices such as the examples given, use the following steps:

1. Determine exactly what student behavior (target behavior) you want to improve.

2. Design and copy the recording sheet you want to use.

3. Make the recording sheets available to your students.

4. Explain to your students exactly what behavior you want them to record, and tell them how you want them to improve.

5. Have the students begin recording and charting their own behavior.

After you have mimeographed enough of the recording sheets or cards for all the students in your class (you could, by the way, have the students make them), tape the sheets or cards on each student's desk. You will need to change these recording forms weekly.

### Figure 9
### Frequency Self-Monitoring Card #1

Make a mark beside each day for each full paragraph you read during reading class.

Monday

Tuesday

Wednesday

Thursday

Friday

Name _____

Week _____

## Figure 10
## Sample Frequency Self-Monitoring Card #2

Make a mark beside each day every time you talk out without permission during math class.

Monday

Tuesday

Wednesday

Thursday

Friday

Name _____

Week _____

After you've given out the forms, explain to the students exactly what behavior they are to record. When you do this it is extremely important to give students clear verbal descriptions of the target behavior, and then role-play examples which represent the behavior and examples which do not represent the behavior. You might, for example, act out or have your students act out, several instances of "talking out without permission," and have the students determine whether each would be recorded. You would then role-play "talking with permission," and quiz the students to be sure that they know the difference between the two types of talking behavior.

## Figure 11
## Sample Frequency Self-Monitoring Card #3

For each day, place a check (✓) each time I give you an
instruction and you follow it immediately.


Monday

Tuesday

Wednesday

Thursday

Friday



Name _____

Week _____

After you're sure your students really know what the behavior is, explain that they will be making a record each time they do
the behavior. This can easily be put in the context of a game.
Make a special point to encourage accuracy in recording, while
also indicating the direction in which you want the target behavior
to change. In other words, clearly tell the students what behavior
you want from them.

While a recording system is being used, you should also teach
the students to chart their recorded data. Teach them to plot the
daily number of occurrences of the target behavior on a graph. So
they can do this, provide each student with a graph (drawn on a
sheet of paper) like the one in Figure 12. The graph should be long
enough to cover a large number of days.

## Figure 12
## Graph for Plotting Behavior Data

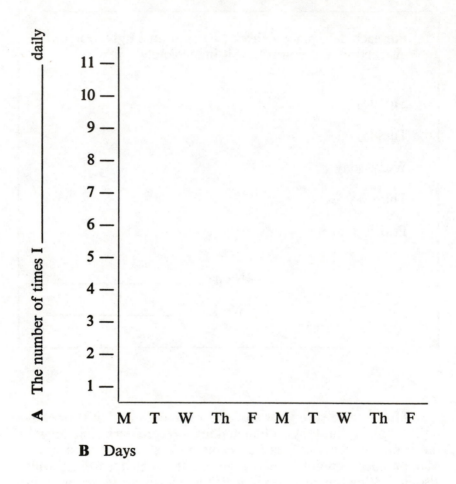

The A side is the number of daily occurrences of the target behavior; the B side represents days. Teach the students to take the total daily frequency of the behavior and plot it over the correct day. Let's look at an example.

Johnny, a fifth grade student, recorded the following daily "frequencies" for the number of math problems he completed during class.

| Monday    | 0 | Monday    | 12 |
|-----------|---|-----------|----|
| Tuesday   | 7 | Tuesday   | 12 |
| Wednesday | 6 | Wednesday | 15 |
| Thursday  | 9 | Thursday  | 14 |
| Friday    | 8 | Friday    | 16 |

To plot his frequencies for each day he placed a dot beside the 0 for Monday, since he completed no problems that day. He placed a dot beside the 7 on Tuesday, beside the 6 on Wednesday, etc. Figure 13 illustrates what Johnny's completed graph would look like.

Notice that in addition to placing dots to plot the frequency of the behavior for each day, lines are drawn from one "data point" to another. This allows students to have clear visual feedback on their progress in controlling their own behavior. The line will trend upward as desirable behaviors increase. The students can see the positive changes that take place.

Let's look at a case study. It involved one of Ms. Clark's tenth grade math classes of twenty-three students. Each day, during the last minutes of the class, the students were given a self-scoring quiz with ten items. A key for scoring the quiz was given each student upon completion of the quiz. These quizzes covered the material dealt with in the previous day's lesson.

Ms. Clark decided to use Frequency Self-Monitoring to help the students improve their motivation and thus their math scores. She wanted them to learn to record and chart the daily number of correct quiz items. After explaining the procedure and its goals, Ms. Clark gave each student an index card on which to record

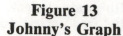

**Figure 13**
**Johnny's Graph**

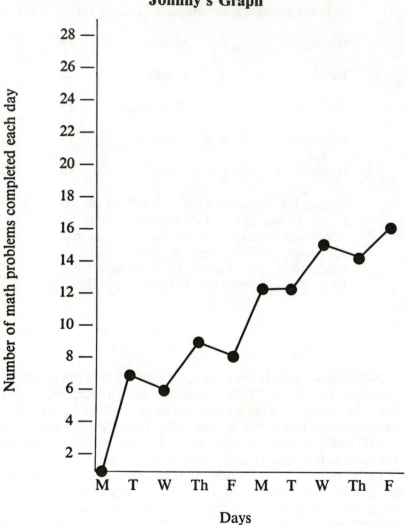

correct items. She also provided each student with a mimeographed chart on which they plotted the day's accomplishments and then returned to her. The results are shown in Figure 14.

**Figure 14**
**Ms. Clark's Frequency Self-Monitoring Program (FSM)**

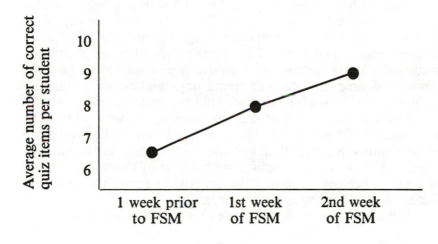

During the week prior to the program the average student in Ms. Clark's math class had approximately 6.5 correct items on the daily math quizzes; at the end of the second week, this was raised to approximately 9 correct items. The results clearly represent a dramatic improvement in the students' math performance. Ms. Clark was so pleased that she decided to make Frequency Self-Monitoring a part of all her math classes.

## INTERVAL SELF-MONITORING

So far, we've only looked at recording and charting with frequency count data. Now, let's explore the other recording method, Interval Self-Monitoring. As you recall, in this method students record whether or not they engaged in a target behavior during a specified interval of time. For example, a student might record whether or not he was on-task (e.g., engaging in schoolwork) during each five-minute interval during a fifty-minute reading class.

Interval Self-Monitoring can be used with any behavior that is continuous rather than discrete. This means that the behavior, by nature, tends to occur over prolonged periods rather than in discrete units. The method is used most often to strengthen students' on-task behaviors. That is, it is used to increase the amount of time that students spend paying attention to instructions and demonstrations and working on assigned tasks.

Implementing Interval Self-Monitoring is very similar to Frequency Self-Monitoring. The primary difference lies in the use of time intervals rather than behavior occurrences as the basis of recording. Instead of recording the number of **times** they engage in a target behavior, the students record the number of **intervals** during which they engage in the behavior.

When teaching students to use this system you must:

1. Determine the time interval: how often the students will record whether or not they are engaging in the target behavior; and

2. Use some method of signalling the end of each time interval so students will know when to record.

As you recall, this is similar to the methods involved in Self-Ratings, part of the Self-Assessment System. The most commonly used interval is five minutes, although you could use intervals ranging from one to ten minutes. With a five minute interval, the students are signalled to record every five minutes. Whenever the signal is given, the students indicate on a recording form whether they have been engaging in the target behavior during the interval. Some examples of Interval Self-Monitoring recording forms are provided in Figures 15 and 16.

**Figure 15**
**Sample Interval Self-Monitoring Form #1**

Each time the signal is given, place a check beside the signal number if you had been working at your desk since the last time you heard the signal.

|         | M  | T  | W  | Th | F  |
|---------|----|----|----|----|----|
| Signal  | 1  | 1  | 1  | 1  | 1  |
|         | 2  | 2  | 2  | 2  | 2  |
|         | 3  | 3  | 3  | 3  | 3  |
|         | 4  | 4  | 4  | 4  | 4  |
|         | 5  | 5  | 5  | 5  | 5  |
|         | 6  | 6  | 6  | 6  | 6  |
|         | 7  | 7  | 7  | 7  | 7  |
|         | 8  | 8  | 8  | 8  | 8  |
|         | 9  | 9  | 9  | 9  | 9  |
|         | 10 | 10 | 10 | 10 | 10 |

Name _____

Week _____

**Figure 16**
**Sample Interval Self-Monitoring Form #2**

Each time you hear the signal circle the number I call out *if* and *only if* you participated in class at least once since you last heard the signal.

|        | M | T | W | Th | F |
|--------|---|---|---|----|---|
| Signal | 1 | 1 | 1 | 1  | 1 |
|        | 2 | 2 | 2 | 2  | 2 |
|        | 3 | 3 | 3 | 3  | 3 |
|        | 4 | 4 | 4 | 4  | 4 |
|        | 5 | 5 | 5 | 5  | 5 |
|        | 6 | 6 | 6 | 6  | 6 |
|        | 7 | 7 | 7 | 7  | 7 |
|        | 8 | 8 | 8 | 8  | 8 |

Name _____

Week _____

The recording signal might be something as simple as ringing a bell or verbally telling the students to record. These require that you frequently watch a clock, however, which can take time away from teaching. An alternative is to use a small kitchen timer. Most timers are reasonably inexpensive and can be set to ring at any interval from one to sixty minutes.

With Frequency Self-Monitoring, students chart their behavior on graphs as well as record it. Interval Self-Monitoring can chart either percentages of intervals on which the behavior occurred, or the number of intervals during which the target behavior occurred. The former should be used only with older students who can compute percentages. Both percentage and number are plotted on the left side of the graph; days, of course, are plotted on the bottom.

Figure 17 shows an Interval Self-Monitoring chart based on percentages. The chart represents one student in a regular eighth grade math class which learned the Interval Self-Monitoring procedure. The target behavior was on-task behavior, defined as sitting in one's seat doing math problems. The interval was five minutes, with a kitchen timer used to signal the end of an interval. At the end of each interval, the students indicated on their recording forms whether they had been on-task as defined. Please note that with younger children, the number of intervals could have been substituted for percentage and the chart would look the same.

As you can see, Interval Self-Monitoring resulted in a rather substantial increase in the student's on-task behavior. Although only the one student was observed, the classroom teacher reported that his improvements were typical for most of the other students in the class.

Let's take a look at another case study. It took place in Mr. Klein's special education resource room. During the period in which the study took place, seven learning disabled children attended for one hour each day. These children ranged in age from seven to ten years, and all were significantly below grade level in reading.

All the students in Mr. Klein's resource room worked with a commercial reading program geared to their individual reading skill levels. Each student was required to read passages, answer questions about the passages, and then draw pictures about what was read.

Concerned with what he saw as an on-task behavior problem, Mr. Klein, with the assistance of the author, implemented an Interval Self-Monitoring program. Every five minutes, Mr. Klein

Percentage of intervals during which you were on-task

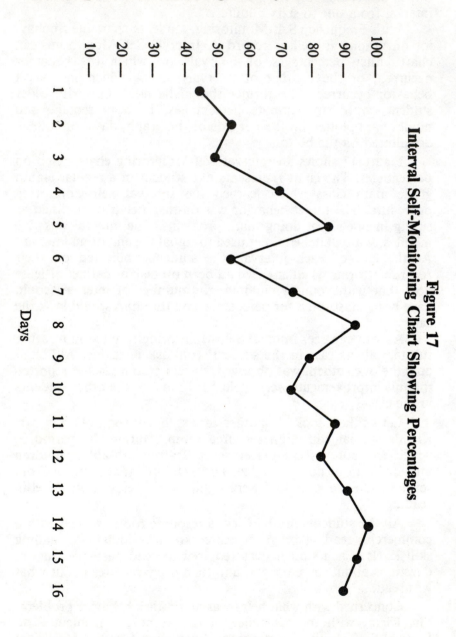

Figure 17
Interval Self-Monitoring Chart Showing Percentages

signalled all students to place a blue self-adhesive sticker on their recording forms which were taped to their table areas. They were to do this if and only if they had been working on the reading task during most of the past five minutes. Students who had not been working during an interval were instructed to skip that interval.

Each of Mr. Klein's seven students was observed for five minutes each day, both one week before the program was implemented and during the third week of the program. The results are shown in Figure 18.

**Figure 18**
**Mr. Klein's Interval Self-Monitoring (ISM) Program**

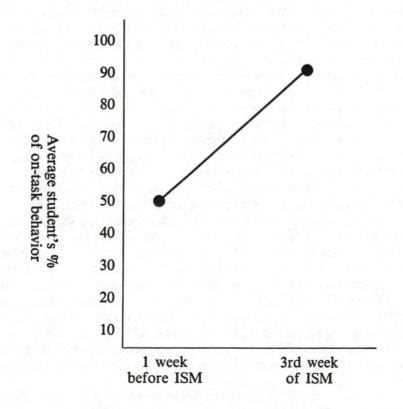

During the week prior to the program, the average student was on-task only about 53% of the time. During the third week, the rate increased to almost 90%, representing an improvement of almost 70%!

## SUMMARY

In this chapter, you have learned to use two Self-Monitoring systems with your students: Frequency Self-Monitoring and Interval Self-Monitoring. As indicated by the research cited in previous chapters, as well as the case studies presented in this chapter, SM procedures can be used with students of widely varying ages and abilities. They appear to be equally useful with elementary, junior high, and high school students and can also be used with students in regular classroom or those in special education resource rooms.

As mentioned in the previous chapters, there may be circumstances when you will want to implement a Phase I behavior modification program for a brief time prior to BSC. If you find that your students have difficulty using Self-Monitoring programs, you could implement a Phase I program for a week and then shift back to an SM program. Experience has indicated that this is usually unnecessary. The vast majority of students have little, if any, difficulty "getting the hang" of SM methods.

Some of you might be wondering how long you should use a SM program. There are two basic ways to address this issue. You could continue the use of SM until the students have reached the desired level of behavior. At that point you might start using the procedure only four days per week. If, after approximately two weeks, the students' behavior gains have been maintained, you might use the procedures only three days per week. After several successful weeks you might start using SM only two days per week. After several more weeks, you might simply give the students an "SM booster" and use the procedures only once per week.

Another approach is to continue to use SM for the whole school year. After all, the procedures will take little of your time, and they will result in substantial improvement in student behavior. What's more, they teach students an extremely important life skill—the ability to manage themselves!

# V

# Self-Reinforcement (SR)

In the previous chapters you learned how to implement Self-Assessment and Self-Monitoring (SM) systems in your classroom. This chapter is about Self-Reinforcement (SR) systems. You will learn how to teach your students to reinforce themselves for appropriate classroom behaviors in order to strengthen those behaviors. As in the previous chapters, you will be provided with step-by-step methods for implementing the procedures and will read about actual case studies of the use of Self-Reinforcement with students.

Two types of Self-Reinforcement will be dealt with in this chapter: Overt Self-Reinforcement and Covert Positive Reinforcement. As you recall from Chapter II, the first involves your students presenting themselves with actual reinforcers, contingent upon appropriate behaviors. Covert Positive Reinforcement involves students systematically imagining themselves receiving reinforcers. The initial sections of the chapter will focus exclusively on Overt Self-Reinforcement procedures since this represents the most often used and best documented SR method. The last section will describe the use of Covert Self-Reinforcement in classroom settings.

# BASIC METHODS OF OVERT
# SELF-REINFORCEMENT

Implementing an overt self-reinforcement program is similar in many ways to the use of Phase I behavior modification techniques. However, one important difference is that the student, not the teacher, administers reinforcers following appropriate behavior.

When implementing an Overt Self-Reinforcement program, the first step is to have your students self-monitor the behavior you want them to improve. To do this, simply implement a Self-Monitoring (SM) system, either Frequency Self-Monitoring or Interval Self-Monitoring, depending on the nature of the behavior. The reason for the use of SM in an Overt Self-Reinforcement program is that your students must, of course, determine whether they have engaged in the target behavior in order to appropriately reinforce themselves for it. SM provides the means for them to do so.

Once you have an SM system in place in your classroom, you can convert it into an Overt Self-Monitoring system by simply informing your students that each time they record a particular behavior, they receive one point or one token. You give values to the recording marks made by the student, which automatically converts such marks into potential reinforcers.

## Using Back-Up Reinforcers

The students' recording marks in and of themselves will probably not serve as reinforcers. In order to turn them into reinforcers you must back up the marks with something of value. To do this, you can set up a system whereby the students can redeem the points or tokens they give themselves for objects or activities which they find desirable. These desirable objects or activities are called back-up reinforcers. Back-up reinforcers are essential for your Overt Self-Reinforcement system to be effective.

To use back-up reinforcers you must make several decisions. The first is whether or not you will allow students to earn different back-up reinforcers or whether all of your students will work for the same "back-ups." You must decide if you will allow individual students to choose their reinforcers.

Allowing individual choice has both advantages and disadvantages. The major advantage is that individual selection insures that the back-up reinforcers are effective. When a student selects the activity or object to work for, it is quite likely that it really is desirable to that student. The major disadvantage of individual selection is that it sometimes poses management problems. Obviously, when students can select their reinforcers, you will have to make a variety of reinforcers available to them and you will have to work out a way to make these reinforcers available *only* when individual students have earned them.

A much more manageable system results when all students have to work for the same reinforcers. You simply set up a single reinforcing activity or object, like 10 minutes extra recess, which all students try to earn. Students earn the reinforcer by obtaining sufficient points; those students who don't earn sufficient points don't receive the extra time.

Although this system is manageable, it is not without a disadvantage. Some students may find your single reinforcer desirable, while others could care less! Those who do not find the activity or object desirable will not work to earn it. As a result, their behavior won't change, because what you're trying to reinforce them with is not reinforcing, and therefore does not motivate them.

### Selecting Reinforcers

The second decision you must make about back-up reinforcers is which ones you will make available. If you plan to allow individual choice, you'll need to select several reinforcers from which students can choose. If you plan to use a single, classroom-wide reinforcer, you'll need to select one which the largest number of your students finds desirable.

Regardless of which method you choose, the best way to determine what would be an effective reinforcer is to ask your students! Many otherwise sound Overt Self-Reinforcement programs fail because the teacher simply assumes that a particular activity is reinforcing to the students, when in fact it is not. Don't make such assumptions. Ask your students to tell you what objects or activities are desirable to them and listen to what they tell you!

The first step in assessing your students' preferences is to make a list of potential reinforcers that you would feel comfortable using. List the objects you have, or can easily get, that students might find reinforcing, and list the activities which you can appropriately allow your students to earn the right to do. When selecting potential reinforcers, try to select ones your students can earn on a daily basis. The more quickly a student can receive the back-up reinforcer, the greater will be its motivational effect.

Once you've made your list of potential reinforcers, either write the list on the board and ask the students to vote on each activity; or mimeograph the list, pass it out, and ask the students to rate each activity. Figure 19 provides an example of a "Reinforcement Menu" that you might mimeograph and pass out.

The reinforcement menu in Figure 19 may or may not include activities or objects which you want to use as reinforcers. No problem! Simply change the menu, inserting the reinforcers you want to use in your Self-Reinforcement program. Regardless of the specific reinforcers you offer, having your students complete the menu will tell you clearly which reinforcers will motivate your students.

Once your students complete a reinforcement menu, you can make some decisions about what to use as back-up reinforcers. If you're only going to use a single classroom-wide reinforcer, it should be something that most students rated in the "really like" category and no students rated in the "don't like" category. If, on the other hand, you plan to allow students to earn different reinforcers, you can use each student's menu as a way to determine what reinforcer will most strongly motivate each student.

## Figure 19
## Sample Reinforcement Menu

Here is a list of several activities you can earn for doing good work in class. Look at each activity and tell me how much YOU like it. If you don't like an activity, put a check in the "DON'T LIKE" space. If you feel that the activity is okay, but not really exciting, put a check in the "OK" space. If you really like an activity, put a check in the "REALLY LIKE" space. Put only one check beside each activity.

| Activity | Don't Like | OK | Really Like |
|----------|------------|-----|-------------|
| 10 Minutes Extra Recess | | | |
| Getting to Talk with a Group of Friends During the Last 10 Minutes of Class | | | |
| Playing _____ During the Last 10 Minutes of Class | | | |
| Reading Comic Books During the Last 15 Minutes of Class | | | |
| Getting to Sit Beside Whomever I Want at Lunch | | | |
| Playing Game _____ During the Last 10 Minutes of Class | | | |
| Winning a "Star Student" Button to Wear | | | |
| Having a Note Sent Home Telling My Parents What Good Work I've Done | | | |

## Connecting Good Behavior and Reinforcement

Once you have determined what back-up reinforcers to use, you will be ready to implement an Overt Self-Reinforcement system. Basically, you have to determine how often the students must engage in the target behavior in order to receive the back-up reinforcer. For example, in order to obtain the reinforcer, must your students be on-task during eight out of twelve five-minute intervals? Or during six out of twelve? Must your students get 75% or 85% of quiz items correct? Must they complete three worksheets with no more than two errors or three worksheets with no more than five errors?

When you set the criterion for obtaining the back-up reinforcer, you must use the principle of successive approximation. In essence, this principle says that initially the criterion for reinforcement should be just slightly higher than the student's current level of behavior. The principle is based on the fact that you can't expect students to make massive changes in a short period of time. Meaningful behavior change must take place in small steps, over time.

When you set your initial criterion for reinforcement, set it just above the target behavior level of the average or most typical student in your class. The way to determine the average student's level of the target behavior is to have the students self-monitor the target behavior for a few days prior to Overt Self-Reinforcement. This will allow you to look at the students' records and quickly determine how often most students engaged in the target behavior. Let's look at an example of this process.

Mr. Wolman had his fifth grade class monitor their on-task behavior during math class. The students recorded whether they were on-task during each of twelve five-minute intervals. When he looked at the students' records after two days, Mr. Wolman found that the majority of students were on-task between four and five intervals out of a possible twelve. Using the principle of successive approximation, Mr. Wolman set the criterion at six. That meant students had to record themselves as being on-task during six of the twelve intervals in order to receive the back-up reinforcer.

Another aspect of the principle of successive approximation is that once most students are consistently reaching the criterion, it should be raised slightly. Mr. Wolman, for example, raised the reinforcement criterion to seven intervals after one week. After two more weeks, he raised it to eight intervals, and so on! The idea is that you're starting out with a criterion that is only slightly different from your students' current behavior. As the students' behavior improves slightly, you can slowly increase the criterion so as to require more improvement.

At this point, you know the general methods and principles required for implementing SR programs in your classroom. In the following sections, we'll look at the specifics of how to implement OSR with various types of classroom behaviors.

## USES OF OVERT SELF-REINFORCEMENT

### Interval Recording

As you learned in Chapter IV, some behaviors, such as on-task behavior, require interval recording. An Overt Self-Reinforcement system implemented to increase such behaviors must be based on an interval recording system. The purpose of such a system is to increase the number of intervals during which the students engage in appropriate target behavior. The system serves to increase the amount of time that students are behaving appropriately.

Let's take a look at the steps involved in using Overt Self-Reinforcement to strengthen classroom behaviors which require interval recording. Notice that the initial steps are identical to those involved in setting up a Self-Monitoring system. This is because, as you learned in the previous section of this chapter, Overt Self-Reinforcement is basically an extension of Self-Monitoring.

**Step 1.** Decide exactly what behaviors you want to increase. Write a description of the target behaviors in very specific terms. Make sure that the behaviors you list are clearly defined and observable so that you and your students know immediately and objectively whether the behavior is occurring at a given moment in time.

**Step 2.** Determine what time interval you will use. How often will your students record whether they engaged in the target behavior? Every five minutes, every ten minutes, etc.?

**Step 3.** Determine how your students will record the target behavior. You must design the form on which students will record.

**Step 4.** Choose the method you will use to signal your students to monitor and record the target behavior. Will you simply announce the end of each interval? Or will you use a mechanical timing device, like a kitchen timer?

**Step 5.** Have your students start monitoring and recording the target behavior. Do this for two to three days.

**Step 6.** Decide what back-up reinforcers you can use to motivate your students. Make a list of them and provide your students with a reinforcement menu. Decide whether there will be only one classroom-wide reinforcer or several reinforcers from which individuals can choose.

**Step 7.** After several days, look at the records of all students in your class. Determine the number of intervals during which most students, or the average students, are engaging in the target behavior.

**Step 8.** Set the criterion for reinforcement just above the number of intervals during which most students are engaging in the target behavior. A 20% or 25% increase over the number of intervals from Step 7 is a good rule of thumb.

**Step 9.** Explain your system clearly. Describe the target behavior and how many intervals of performing the target behavior the students must have in order to get the back-up reinforcer(s). Also, tell your students why they're going to use the system, what target behavior will be increased.

**Step 10.** Implementing the system. Instruct the students to show you their records. Whenever a student reaches criterion, either (1) award the back-up reinforcer immediately, or (2) place the student's name on the board to indicate that the student will receive the reinforcer during the designated reinforcement time.

**Step 11.** If your informal monitoring suggests it is necessary, implement a procedure to increase the accuracy of the students' records. (See Chapter II.)

**Step 12.** When most students are consistently reaching the criterion for one or two full weeks increase the criterion slightly.

**Step 13.** Periodically re-administer a reinforcement menu to insure that the reinforcers you're using remain desirable. If your students' preferences have changed, change the reinforcers you're using.

**Step 14.** Periodically tell your principal about the fabulous success you're having in teaching self-control skills to your students. This will provide you will some social reinforcement!

Now let's take a look at some case studies which show how Overt Self-Reinforcement can be used in actual classrooms to increase student behaviors.

Ms. Walters had a class of twenty-six fourth grade students whose average math skill level was 3.2 (second month of third grade). She concluded that the students' math performance could be improved by increasing their on-task behavior.

Ms. Walters wrote the following definition of on-task behavior on a chart and placed it in front of the classroom for all students to see:

On-Task Behavior Means:

1. sitting in one's seat working math problems,

2. following the lecture in the textbook, and

3. watching the teacher demonstrate a problem on the board.

Ms. Walters decided to use a five-minute interval and placed an egg timer on her desk so she would know when to announce the end of each interval. The recording form shown in Figure 20 was taped on the students' desks each week.

The students in Ms. Walter's classroom monitored their on-task behavior for three days during math class. At the end of the math period on the third day, Ms. Walters checked each student's recording form to find the number of intervals on which the average student was on-task. Since this was six intervals, the reinforcement criterion was set at seven intervals.

An Overt-Self-Reinforcement program was implemented the following day. A reinforcement menu indicated that fifteen minutes of extra recess was a highly desirable activity for all students in the class. Students who were on-task for seven intervals had their names placed on the board, indicating they would receive the reinforcer.

The criterion of seven intervals was in effect for two weeks. Over the next several weeks it was increased to eight and then to nine intervals. The results of Ms. Walters' program are shown in Figure 21.

**Figure 20**
**Math Self-Recording Form**

Name _____

Week _____

### Math Self-Recording Form

Each time I announce the end of a five-minute period, I want you to think about whether you were on-task during that period. If so, place a check beside the number I announce.

| M | T | W | Th | F |
|---|---|---|----|---|
| 1 | 1 | 1 | 1 | 1 |
| 2 | 2 | 2 | 2 | 2 |
| 3 | 3 | 3 | 3 | 3 |
| 4 | 4 | 4 | 4 | 4 |
| 5 | 5 | 5 | 5 | 5 |
| 6 | 6 | 6 | 6 | 6 |
| 7 | 7 | 7 | 7 | 7 |
| 8 | 8 | 8 | 8 | 8 |
| 9 | 9 | 9 | 9 | 9 |
| 10 | 10 | 10 | 10 | 10 |

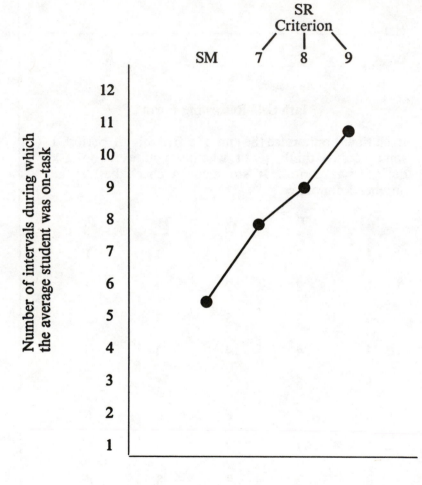

**Figure 21**
**Ms. Walters' Overt Self-Reinforcement Program (OSR)**

The graph of the students' behavior clearly shows the increase in on-task behavior associated with the program. During the three days that Self-Monitoring was used, the average student was on-task only during approximately 5.5 intervals. By the time the reinforcement criterion had been raised to nine intervals, seven weeks after OSR began, the average student was on task during 10.5 intervals. Perhaps more important is the fact that at the end of the year the average student's math skill level was on par with that expected for his or her grade. Apparently, the increase in on-task behavior resulted in increased learning!

In another case study, Mr. Pruitt had a class of 22 third grade students, most of whom were below grade level in reading. He implemented an Overt Self-Reinforcement program in order to increase the amount of time his students spent working on independent, in-class reading assignments.

Mr. Pruitt gave the students a blue cup containing white plastic chips and an empty red cup. Both cups were taped on each student's desk. A kitchen timer rang at the end of ten five-minute intervals. Mr. Pruitt had taught the students to move one of their white plastic chips from the blue cup to the red cup if and only if they had been working on their reading assignment when the bell rang.

A reinforcement menu had isolated several classroom activities which the students wanted to learn. These involved playing with various puzzles and games. Mr. Pruitt set up a contingency wherein the students could earn two minutes of "free time" to play with these activities for every white chip they had in their red cups at the end of reading period. The "free time" took place immediately following reading period.

The results of Mr. Pruitt's program are shown in Figure 22. Figure 22 clearly indicates the positive changes in the students' behavior. At the beginning of the program, the average student was "on-task" for only about 2.4 intervals. After seven weeks, that increased to eight intervals. Mr. Pruitt also reported a marked improvement in the reading quiz scores of most students.

## Academic Product Behaviors

In the previous section you learned to implement an Overt Self-Reinforcement system designed to increase the amount of time (i.e., the number of intervals) that students engage in behaviors believed to result in improved performance. You learned to indirectly improve student performance by strengthening interval behaviors, in this case on-task behavior, assumed to be directly related to task performance. In this section, you'll learn to use the technique to directly improve student performance on various tasks. We'll focus on teaching students to reinforce themselves to increase certain academic product behaviors.

## Figure 22
## Mr. Pruitt's Overt Self-Reinforcement Program (OSR)

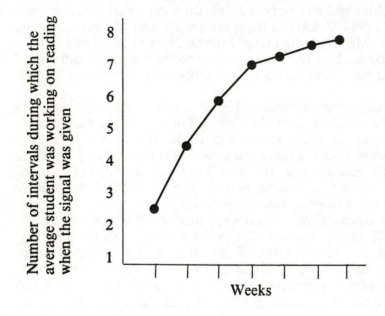

Number of intervals during which the average student was working on reading when the signal was given

Weeks

Below are the steps involved in using Overt Self-Reinforcement with academic product behaviors. Notice that the steps are similar, and in some cases identical, to those in the previous section.

**Step 1.** Determine what specific academic performance you want to improve. Do you want to increase the number of correct items on quizzes? The number of paragraphs read during in-class reading assignments? The number of math problems worked correctly?

**Step 2.** Once the target academic behavior is selected, you must devise a form for the students to use to record their performance.

**Step 3.** Place the recording form on your students' desks, tell them how to record their performance, and have them use Self-Monitoring for several days. If the target performance involves the number of correct responses on a task, provide the students with a scoring key in order to compute the number of correct responses.

**Step 4.** Determine what back-up reinforcers to use with your particular group of students.

**Step 5.** After several days, look at the students' records to determine the typical student's current level of performance on the target behavior.

**Step 6.** Set the criterion for reinforcement about 20% above the performance level from step 5.

**Step 7.** Describe the complete system to your students. Specify the criterion (e.g., number of correct responses on quizzes, number of paragraphs read, etc.) for the reinforcer(s) and tell the students when they will have access to the reinforcers.

**Step 8.** Implement the system. Increase the criterion for reinforcement as the students' performance improves.

**Step 9.** If necessary, implement a surveillance system (as described in Chapter II) to increase accuracy.

**Step 10.** Periodically re-administer the reinforcement menu to insure that the "reinforcers" remain effective.

Here are some case studies which exemplify the use of Overt Self-Reinforcement to improve academic product behaviors.

Ms. Stall had a regular class of twenty-four junior high school students, many of whom were performing poorly in math. Her own analysis of the situation indicated that all the students had the ability to do the math problems, but they seemed to lack motivation.

Ms. Stall decided to use an Overt Self-Reinforcement program in order to increase the number of problems the students correctly completed on daily math assignments. She devised the form shown in Figure 23, and helped each student tape it to the inside back cover of their math notebooks. The students were given access to one of several copies of the assignment scoring key. They were required to score their assignments at Ms. Stall's desk and then turn them in. A surveillance system was in effect throughout the program.

After one week of student Self-Monitoring, Ms. Stall implemented an Overt Self-Reinforcement program. Any student who recorded fifteen or more correct items received ten minutes of free time that could be "cashed in" at the end of the math period on the following day. A "free time area" was designated in the back of the classroom where students could talk quietly, read comics or magazines, etc.

After three weeks, Ms. Stall increased the reinforcement criterion to nineteen or more items. The results of this program are shown in Figure 24.

Figure 23 clearly demonstrates the effectiveness of Self-Reinforcement in improving Ms. Stall's students' math performance. The average student went from twelve correct items to almost nineteen correct items within seven weeks. This represents an improvement of 58%!

## Figure 23
## Sample Overt Self-Reinforcement Recording Form

Name _____

Week _____

### Math Success Form

Circle the number of problems you correctly solve on each daily assignment. Use the key to score your assignments.

| Monday | 1 | 2 | 3 | 4 | 5 | 6 | 7 | 8 | 9 | 10 |
|---|---|---|---|---|---|---|---|---|---|---|
|  | 11 | 12 | 13 | 14 | 15 | 16 | 17 | 18 | 19 | 20 |
| Tuesday | 1 | 2 | 3 | 4 | 5 | 6 | 7 | 8 | 9 | 10 |
|  | 11 | 12 | 13 | 14 | 15 | 16 | 17 | 18 | 19 | 20 |
| Wednesday | 1 | 2 | 3 | 4 | 5 | 6 | 7 | 8 | 9 | 10 |
|  | 11 | 12 | 13 | 14 | 15 | 16 | 17 | 18 | 19 | 20 |
| Thursday | 1 | 2 | 3 | 4 | 5 | 6 | 7 | 8 | 9 | 10 |
|  | 11 | 12 | 13 | 14 | 15 | 16 | 17 | 18 | 19 | 20 |
| Friday | 1 | 2 | 3 | 4 | 5 | 6 | 7 | 8 | 9 | 10 |
|  | 11 | 12 | 13 | 14 | 15 | 16 | 17 | 18 | 19 | 20 |

**Figure 24**
**Ms. Stall's Overt Self-Reinforcement Program (OSR)**

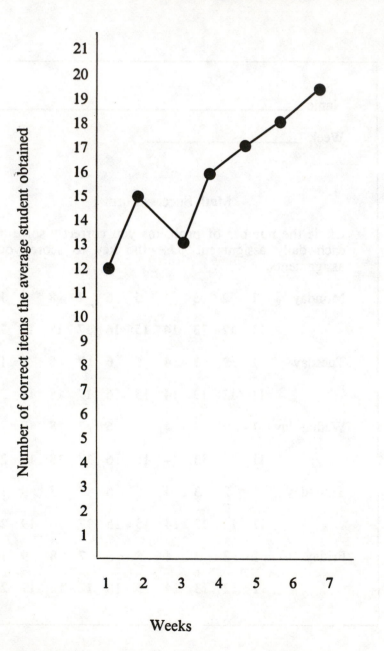

Mr. Abbot's class of twenty-three third graders was doing poorly on reading assignments. Since the screening component of the new reading program indicated that all the students had the skills to perform successfully, he decided to increase the students' motivation through an Overt Self-Reinforcement program. Specifically, he wanted to increase the number of reading comprehension questions the students could answer correctly on daily quizzes.

Since the school's reading program provided answer sheets for quizzes, Mr. Abbot simply had the students score their quizzes with the key and write the number they answered correctly on the top of the answer sheets. Although the students were allowed to keep their answer sheets as records of their progress, Mr. Abbot checked the quizzes for accuracy twice per week.

After administering a reinforcement menu, Mr. Abbot implemented the Self-Reinforcement program. Any student who correctly answered at least eight of the ten daily quiz questions could choose between (1) ten minutes of extra recess that afternoon, or (2) having a mimeographed note sent home indicating the student's achievements in reading.

The results of Mr. Abbot's program are shown in Figure 25. Quite clearly, Figure 25 indicates the dramatic effects the program had on Mr. Abbot's students' performance. The average number of correct items for an average student increased from about four to about eight over a six-week period.

## Decreasing Inappropriate Behaviors

In the previous sections, we examined the use of Overt Self-Reinforcement to increase various types of appropriate behavior. It can also be used to decrease certain inappropriate classroom behaviors, like disruptive actions.

You know that if a behavior is reinforced, through OSR for example, it will increase in strength. However, not only will the behavior become stronger, but behaviors that are incompatible with the reinforced behavior will decrease! Let's take the example of the following class of on-task behaviors: quietly sitting in one's seat, working on a math assignment and quietly sitting in one's seat, watching the teacher work a problem. Obviously, two inappropriate behaviors, in particular, are incompatible with the

### Figure 25
## Mr. Abbot's Overt Self-Reinforcement Program (OSR)

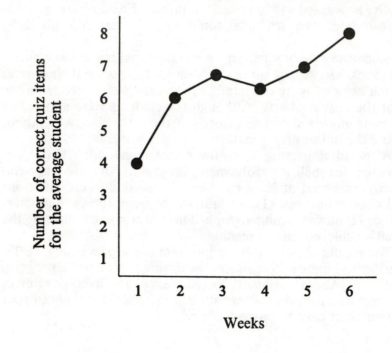

above on-task behavior. They are out-of-seat and talking-out behaviors. These behaviors are incompatible because a student cannot be both on-task and engaging in out-of-seat or talking-out behavior. It follows that if the on-task behaviors increase, then the out-of-seat and talking-out behaviors must decrease.

The principle of incompatible behavior allows you to use Overt Self-Reinforcement to decrease inappropriate behaviors. The key is to be sure that when you select and define a behavior to be increased, you do it in a way that is incompatible with inappropriate behaviors. This way you will "lock in" a relation between the behaviors in question that will allow you to "kill two birds with one stone," increase the appropriate behavior while simultaneously decreasing incompatible inappropriate behaviors.

Let's take a look at a case study where Overt Self-Reinforcement was used to decrease disruptive behaviors. Ms. Castle was the special education/resource teacher for a group of eight high school students ranging in age from fifteen to eighteen. All had severe deficits in reading and math achievement. The average student's "delay" in reading was five years, and the average delay in math was seven years. The students were in Ms. Castle's class for one hour each day.

Concerned with a high rate of talking-out and out-of-seat behavior in her class, Ms. Castle sought the author's assistance in designing a Behavioral Self-Control program. Due to a belief that her students would have difficulty initially with an Overt Self-Reinforcement program, a traditional Phase I behavior modification program was implemented for two weeks. In this program, the students received one point for each of three thirteen-minute periods in which they remained in their seats, talked only to ask Ms. Castle questions about the assignment, and completed at least one page of the assignment workbook. These behaviors were considered incompatible with the disruptive behaviors Ms. Castle wanted to decrease.

During the first week of the Phase I program, students receiving at least two points received ten minutes of free time at the end of the class period. During the second week, three points were required to earn the ten-minute free time period.

After two weeks of the Phase I program, Ms. Castle implemented an Overt Self-Reinforcement procedure. The students monitored their own behavior every thirteen minutes, as signalled by Ms. Castle, and gave themselves one point when they engaged in the target behaviors described above. As in the Phase I program, these points earned free time. The results of this program after two weeks are shown in Figure 26.

During the week prior to the Phase I behavior modification program, the average student engaged in approximately 6.8 disruptive behaviors per day. During the Phase I program, this was reduced to an average of approximately 2.8 disruptive behaviors per day. During the first two weeks of the Overt Self-Reinforcement program, the rate was further reduced to approximately one disruptive behavior per day.

**Figure 26**
**Ms. Castle's Overt Self-Reinforcement Program (OSR)**

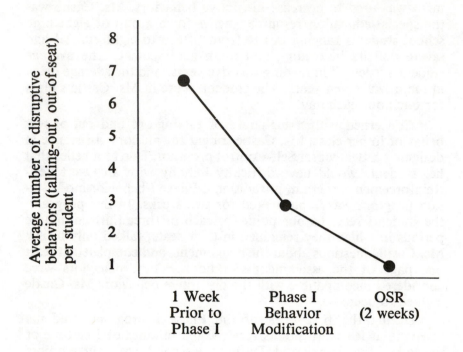

## COVERT POSITIVE REINFORCEMENT

In recent years, behavioral researchers have developed BSC procedures which capitalize on something at which many students are quite adept—daydreaming. You didn't misunderstand! Some contemporary procedures actually use students' fantasies to improve their behavior. These procedures are called covert conditioning (Cautela, 1970; Workman & Dickinson, 1979; Workman & Dickinson, 1980).

One of the most commonly used covert conditioning procedures is called Covert Positive Reinforcement. This procedure involves having a student imagine the following things:

1. being in a situation where a certain appropriate behavior is needed, like when the teacher gives an in-class math assignment,

2. engaging in the appropriate behavior, and experiencing a highly positive/pleasurable scene.

In Covert Positive Reinforcement the highly positive scene serves as a reinforcer for the appropriate behavior imagined by the student. The result is that the imagined appropriate behavior is strengthened in the classroom (Workman & Dickinson, 1979 and 1980).

To implement a Covert Positive Reinforcement program in your classroom, you must first determine several reinforcers to use in the positive scenes. Bear in mind that since the students will be imagining the reinforcers, you do not have to offer reinforcers that you can actually give. The best way to assess the most effective covert reinforcers is to ask each student to make a list of ten events they really like. As a prompt you might offer five or six examples, such as eating a hamburger at a popular fast food chain, receiving a favorite toy or hobby item, going to visit a television movie star, etc. Your examples, of course, should be in line with your students' ages.

When the students have completed their lists, collect and examine them. Try to extract at least five activities which are listed by all students. Once you have isolated five or more you are ready to start implementing a Covert Positive Reinforcement program in your class. Use the following three steps:

**Step 1.** Tell your students to imagine themselves in the situation where you want their behavior to improve. For example, you might say, "I want everyone to close your eyes and imagine yourself in this class. Now imagine that I am telling you to take out your reading workbooks to do the assignment."

**Step 2.** Then, have your students imagine themselves successfully engaging in a behavior that is appropriate to the above classroom situation. For example, "Now imagine yourselves taking out your workbook and really working hard on the reading assignment. Be sure that you keep your eyes closed and imagine this as clearly as possible."

**Step 3.** During the final step, instruct your students to imagine one of the highly positive events from their lists. For example, "Now, imagine yourself getting to meet all the stars of your favorite television show. Imagine that you're really excited, and the stars are all talking with you and being friendly."

When you use the three steps above each should be followed immediately by the next step, and each should last at least twenty seconds in order for the procedure to be effective. You might have your students raise their hands (or their pointer fingers) as soon as they can clearly visualize an image. This will allow you to approximate a twenty second duration for each image.

When using Covert Positive Reinforcement, take your students through the three steps five to ten times per day. Whenever you give the instructions for Step 3, alternate the different reinforcers selected by your students. This will keep your students from becoming satiated on a single reinforcement scene.

As you achieve some success, reduce the frequency of the program. For example, instead of continuing with five to ten trials per day, reduce the number to two or three trials carried out three days per week.

Let's examine a case study demonstrating the use of Covert Positive Reinforcement. The students in this case study were twenty-one fifth grade students in a regular social studies class. The classroom teacher, Ms. Wilson, wanted to increase the students' on-task behavior. So, with the assistance of the author, she implemented a Covert Positive Reinforcement program for two weeks.

Each day, Ms. Wilson instructed the students, as a group, to imagine the following sequence.

1. Ms. Wilson is giving an assignment for in-class completion,

2. I am working diligently on the social studies assignment, and

3. I am experiencing (one of several highly reinforcing events described by Ms. Wilson).

Ms. Wilson had her students imagine the above sequence five times each morning at the beginning of class. The results of this case study are shown in Figure 27.

**Figure 27**
**Ms. Wilson's Covert Positive Reinforcement Program**
**(CPR)**

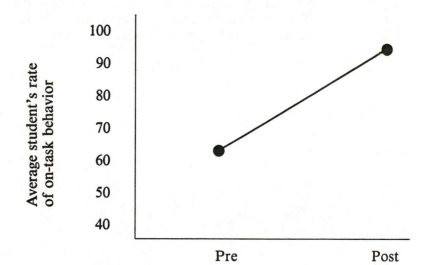

The results shown in Figure 27 are based on observations of five randomly selected students from Ms. Wilson's class. On the day before the program was implemented, the average student's rate of on-task behavior was approximately 63%. When observations were taken three days after the termination of the program, the average students' on-task behavior had increased to almost 90%.

## SUMMARY

In this chapter, we've explored the various uses of both Overt Self-Reinforcement and Covert Positive Reinforcement to improve classroom behavior. You can now add Self-Reinforcement to your repertoire of skills for improving students' process and academic product behaviors.

At this point, you may be wondering when to use Self-Reinforcement (SR) instead of Self-Monitoring (SM) or some other BSC procedure. Certainly, all of the procedures we have examined so far have merit. In choosing one over another, think primarily in terms of (1) what procedure you believe your students will be more likely to accept, and (2) your own personal style. If one procedure does not yield the effects you desire, add other procedures or try a different procedure altogether. Remember, the essence of a truly rational approach to improving student behavior is trial and error. Try a procedure, and if it works, great! If not, modify it or try another until you get the results you want.

# VI

# Conclusion

This book has exposed the reader to the rationale for Behavioral Self Control and the three major types of BSC. Chapter I explored the overall rationale for teaching BSC to students. Although you can probably think of many reasons why it is desirable for students to learn self-control skills, the book focused on the three that the author believes to be of prime importance.

One rationale for teaching BSC is the belief that it provides students with the means to cope with a world characterized by inconsistent and delayed behavioral feedback. Since the "real world" outside the classroom does not usually provide clear and consistent feedback, the student, in the process of maturing, must learn to guide his own behavior, at least to some extent. BSC represents one effective means for learning to provide oneself with behavior "self-guidance."

A second rationale lies in the possibility of encouraging students to take responsibility for their own behavior. We discussed this issue in the context of the concept of **locus of control**. As you remember, people with an internal locus of control see themselves as being the primary cause of whatever happens to them. They thus tend to take responsibility for their own behavior and are likely to be well-motivated, since they view themselves as being capable of influencing their own destiny. There exists some evidence that BSC tends to foster an internal locus of control, and therefore represents a means of teaching "self-responsibility."

The final rationale for teaching BSC involved the need to foster maintenance and generalization of positive behavior changes. You remember that maintenance refers to the durability of behavior improvements, while generalization refers to the transfer of behavior improvements from one situation to another. Several studies suggesting that BSC enhances both generalization and maintenance were discussed.

After covering the rationale for teaching BSC, Chapter I explored the various classroom behaviors BSC can improve, including on-task behavior, disruptive behaviors, and academic product behaviors.

In the final section of Chapter I you learned that there are three basic BSC processes: Self-Assessment, Self-Monitoring, and Self-Reinforcement.

Chapter II explored basic principles and techniques of BSC in some detail. You saw that Self-Assessment processes yield three distinct techniques: Self-Rating, Self-Instruction Training, and Verbal Mediation Training. Self-Monitoring yields the techniques of Frequency and Interval Self-Monitoring. Two techniques based on Self-Reinforcement principles were also discussed: Overt Self-Reinforcement and Covert Positive Reinforcement. A number of studies demonstrating the efficacy of these techniques were described.

The latter sections of Chapter II dealt with two important issues in the use of BSC, namely the need for prior experience with Phase I procedures and the accuracy of students' self-monitoring and reinforcement. In terms of the former, evidence was presented that BSC can be effectively used without initially exposing students to traditional Phase I programs. However, it was pointed out that if you feel your students need such exposure, you can readily implement a brief Phase I period just prior to the implementation of BSC.

In terms of the accuracy of students' self-monitoring and self-reinforcement, it was noted that accuracy is usually not a problem in BSC programs. However, in case your students do have such difficulties, two methods for increasing accuracy were presented: reinforcement for accurate recording and the illusion of intense surveillance.

Chapters III, IV, and V presented procedures for implementing programs based on Self-Assessment, Self-Monitoring, and Self-Reinforcement, respectively. For each BSC technique, you were provided with detailed instructions for implementation. Case studies were also presented in order to show how the various BSC techniques actually operate in classroom settings.

When implementing BSC programs (or, for that matter, any behavior change program), remember that the most important factor for success is consistency. Even the most potentially effective programs will fail if their implementation is erratic and inconsistent. Once you implement a BSC program, you must stick with it! Don't use BSC one day and then forget about it until next week. Be sure to continue a program every day until your students have achieved the level of success you desire. At that point you may begin Phase II, the fading of formal procedures, while allowing the natural environment to maintain behavior improvements.

# References

Bandura, A. *Social learning theory*. Englewood Cliffs, NJ: Prentice-Hall, 1977.

Blackwood, R. The operant conditioning of verbally mediated self-control in the classroom. *Journal of School Psychology*, 1970, *8*, 251-258.

Bolstad, O., & Johnson, S. Self-regulation in the modification of disruptive classroom behavior. *Journal of Applied Behavior Analysis*, 1972, *5*, 443-454.

Borstein, P., & Quevillon, R. The effects of a self-instructional package on overactive preschool boys. *Journal of Applied Behavior Analysis*, 1976, *9*, 179-188.

Bradley, R., & Gaa, J. Domain specific aspects of locus of control: Implications for modifying locus of control orientation. *Journal of School Psychology*, 1977, *15*, 18-24.

Cautela, J. Covert reinforcement. *Behavior Therapy*, 1970, *1*, 33-50.

Clarizio, H. *Toward positive classroom discipline*. New York: John Wiley and Sons, 1980.

Gagne, R. *The conditions of learning*. New York: Holt, Rinehart, and Winston, 1965.

Glynn, E. Classroom applications of self-determined reinforcement. *Journal of Applied Behavior Analysis*, 1970, *3*, 123-132.

Glynn, E., Thomas, J., & Shee, S. Behavioral self-control of on-task behavior in an elementary school classroom. *Journal of Applied Behavior Analysis*, 1973, *6*, 105-113.

Humphrey, L., & Karoly, P. Self-management in the classroom. Self-imposed response cost versus self-reward. *Behavior Therapy*, 1978, *9*, 592-601.

Hundert, J., & Bastone, D. A practical procedure to maintain pupils' accurate self-rating in a classroom token program. *Behavior Modification*, 1978, *2*, 93-112.

Kaufman, K., & O'Leary, K. Reward, cost, and self-evaluation procedures for disruptive adolescents in a psychiatric hospital school. *Journal of Applied Behavior Analysis*, 1972, *5*, 293-309.

Kazdin, A. *Behavior modification in applied settings*. Homewood, Il.: The Dorsey Press, 1980.

Kendall, P. On the efficacious use of verbal self-instruction procedures with children. *Cognitive Therapy and Research*, 1977, *1*, 331-341.

Litrownik, A., Freitas, J., & Franzini, L. Self-regulation in mentally retarded children: Assessment and training of self-monitoring skills. *American Journal of Mental Deficiency*, 1978, *82*, 499-506.

Long, J., & Frye, V. *Wait until Friday*. Princeton Book Co., 1977.

Marholin, D., & Steinman, W. Stimulus control in the classroom as a function of the behavior reinforced. *Journal of Applied Behavior Analysis*, 1977, *10*, 465-478.

Mahoney, M., & Mahoney, K. Self-control techniques with the mentally retarded. *Exceptional Children*, 1976, *42*, 338-339.

Meichenbaum, D., & Goodman, J. Training impulsive children to talk to themselves: A means of developing self control. *Journal of Abnormal Psychology*, 1971, *77*, 115-126.

Moletzky, B. Behavior recording as treatment: A brief note. *Behavior Therapy*, 1974, *5* 107-111.

O'Leary, K., Becker, W., Evans, M., & Saudargas, S. A token reinforcement program in a public school: A replication and systematic analysis. *Journal of Applied Behavior Analysis*, 1969, *2*, 3-13.

Pawlicki, R. Effects of self-directed modification training on a measure of locus of control. *Psychological Reports*, 1976, *39*, 319-322.

Piersel, W., & Kratochwill, T. Self-observation and behavior change: Applications to academic and adjustment problems through behavioral consultation. *Journal of School Psychology*, 1979, *17*, 151-161.

Wahler, R., House, A., & Stambaugh, E. *Ecological assessment of child problem behavior*. New York: Pergamon Press, 1976.

Walker, H. *The acting-out child*. Boston: Allyn and Bacon, 1979.

Walker, H., & Buckley, N. Programming generalization and maintenance of treatment effects across time and across settings. *Journal of Applied Behavior Analysis*, 1972, *5*, 209-224.

Williams, R., & Anandam, K. *Cooperative classroom management*. Columbus, OH: Merrill Publishing Co., 1973.

Williams, R., & Long, J. *Toward a self-managed life style*. New York: Houghton-Mifflin, 1979.

Wood, R., & Flynn, J. A self-evaluation token system vs. an external token system alone in a residential setting with predelinquent youth. *Journal of Applied Behavior Analysis*, 1978, *11*, 503-512.

Workman, E., & Dickinson, D. The use of covert positive reinforcement in the treatment of a hyperactive child. An empirical case study. *Journal of School Psychology*. 1979, *17*, 57-73.

Workman E., & Dickinson, D. The use of covert conditioning with children: Three empirical case studies. *Education and Treatment of Children*, 1980, *2*, 24-36.

Workman, E., & Hector, M. Behavior self control in classroom settings: A review of the literature. *Journal of School Psychology*, 1978, *16*, 227-236.

Workman, E., Helton, G., & Watson, P. Self-monitoring effects in a four year old child: An ecological behavior analysis. *Journal of School Psychology*, 1982, *20*, in press.

# Appendix
# Glossary of BSC Techniques

**Self-Assessment** (SA): the component of BSC where students learn to evaluate their own behavior.

*Self-Rating:* a SA technique where students are taught to rate their behavior on a scale provided by the teacher. Self-Ratings can be used to increase on-task and decrease disruptive behavior.

*Self-Instruction Training:* a SA technique where students learn to guide their own behavior by verbally prompting or cueing themselves to perform a task in a particular manner. It is primarily used to increase on-task behavior and decrease the frequency of careless errors.

*Verbal Mediation Training:* a SA procedure in which students write essays answering questions about their rule-violations. It is used primarily to decrease disruptive behavior.

**Self-Monitoring** (SM): the component of BSC where students are taught to monitor and record their own behavior.

*Frequency Self-Monitoring:* a SM technique in which students record the number of times they engage in a certain behavior each day. It can be used to increase the number of assignments completed by students and the number of correct student response on assignments. It can also be used to decrease disruptive behaviors as long as such behaviors are strongly discouraged in the classroom.

*Interval Self-Monitoring:* a SM technique in which students record the number of time intervals during which they engage in a certain behavior. It can be used to increase on-task behavior.

**Self-Reinforcement** (SR): the component of BSC in which students are taught to reward themselves for engaging in appropriate behaviors.

*Overt Self-Reinforcement:* a SR technique where students give themselves points or tokens (exchangeable for reinforcers) contingent upon appropriate behavior. It can be used to increase on-task behaviors and academic product behaviors. It can also be used to decrease disruptive behaviors.

*Covert Positive Reinforcement:* a SR technique in which students learn to use fantasies to reward themselves for appropriate behaviors. It can be used to increase on-task behaviors and decrease disruptive behaviors.

# Index